FOOD EDITOR: Pamela Clark

ASSOCIATE FOOD EDITOR: Karen Hammial

ASSISTANT FOOD EDITORS: Lucy Kelly, Louise Patniotis

HOME ECONOMISTS: Emma Braz, Kimberley Coverdale, Nadia French, Sarah Hobbs, Justin Kerr, Kathy McGarry, Sarah O'Brien, Maria Sampsonis, Jodie Tilse, Amal Webster, Lovoni Welch

EDITORIAL COORDINATOR: Elizabeth Hooper

KITCHEN ASSISTANT: Amy Wong

• • •

ART DIRECTOR: Sue de Guingand

DESIGNER: Caryl Wiggins

STYLISTS: Carolyn Fienberg, Kay Francis, Jane Hann, Jacqui Hing, Cherise Koch, Sophia Young

PHOTOGRAPHERS: Robert Clark, Robert Taylor

• • •

HOME LIBRARY STAFF

EDITOR-IN-CHIEF: Mary Coleman

ART DIRECTOR: Sue de Guingand

DESIGNER: Caryl Wiggins

ASSISTANT EDITOR: Lynne Smith

EDITORIAL COORDINATOR: Lee Stephenson

• • •

MANAGING DIRECTOR: Colin Morrison

GROUP PUBLISHER: Tim Trumper

• • •

Produced by The Australian Women's Weekly Home Library. Colour separations by ACP Colour Graphics Pty Ltd, Sydney. Printing by Hannanprint, Sydney. Published by ACP Publishing Pty. Limited, 54 Park Street, Sydney; GPO Box 4088, Sydney, NSW 1028, (02) 9282 8000.
◆ AUSTRALIA: Distributed by Network Distribution Company, 54 Park Street, Sydney, NSW 2000, (02) 9282 8777.
◆ UNITED KINGDOM: Distributed in the UK by Australian Consolidated Press (UK) Ltd, 20 Galowhill Rd, Brackmills, Northampton NN4 7EE, (01604) 760 456.
◆ CANADA: Distributed in Canada by Whitecap Books Ltd, 351 Lynn Ave, North Vancouver, BC V7J 2C4, (604) 980 9852.
◆ NEW ZEALAND: Distributed in New Zealand by Netlink Distribution Company, 17B Hargreaves St, Level 5, College Hill, Auckland 1, (9) 302 7616.
◆ SOUTH AFRICA: Distributed in South Africa by Intermag, PO Box 57394, Springfield 2137, Johannesburg, (011) 491 7534.

• • •

All-time Favourites from The Australian Women's Weekly
Includes index.
ISBN 1 86396 058 9

1. Cookery. (Series: Australian Women's Weekly Home Library).

641.5

• • •

FRONT COVER: Creme Caramel, *above*, page 42; Festive Fruit and Nut Cake, *below*, page 104.
BACK COVER: Creamy Marinara Pasta, *above*, and Tomato Marinara Pasta, *below*, page 20.
OPPOSITE: Spinach, Bacon and Fetta Pizza; Mushroom Pizza; The Deli-Delight Pizza, *clockwise from top*.
RIGHT: Fettuccine Carbonara, page 32.

ALL-TIME FAVOURITES

from THE AUSTRALIAN WOMEN'S WEEKLY

It gives us great pleasure to introduce this book to you because it's one you've asked for time and time again – all the recipes we've published which, over the years, have become much-loved favourites appear here within the covers of a single volume. No more searching through recipe drawers or huge stacks of magazines: just reach for **All-time Favourites** and you're on your way to a meal (or a spectacular cake) guaranteed to make your friends and family grow faint with pleasure... our family here in the Test Kitchen is equally pleased to have satisfied your many requests so simply and beautifully.

Pamela Clark

FOOD EDITOR

BRITISH & NORTH AMERICAN READERS: Please note that Australian cup and spoon measurements are metric. A quick conversion guide appears on page 127. A glossary explaining unfamiliar terms and ingredients appears on page 122.

Rich Christmas Pudding, page 94.

Apricot Lemon Processor Marmalade, page 82.

Triple Choc Brownies, page 76.

Contents

Roast Sirloin of Beef with Horseradish Seasoning, page 21.

Best Caesar Salad, page 39.

Supreme Cottage Loaf, page 32.

The Famous Test Kitchen

Pamela Clark, above centre, with three Home Economists from the Test Kitchen, from left, Emma Braz, Maria Sampsonis and Nadia French.

Since 1976, The Australian Women's Weekly Home Library Test Kitchen has researched, tested, photographed and produced more than 70 full-length cookbooks which have combined sales of over 30 million copies, published into 18 different languages, worldwide.

Food Editor Pamela Clark and a staff of home economists create every recipe, then triple-test each one for guaranteed success, ease of preparation, accessibility of ingredients... and great taste.

Soups & Starters

These beautiful beginners impressively create a mood of excitement for a meal and, when partnered with a crusty loaf of fresh bread, they also quickly assume the starring role in a special lunch or late-night supper. Talented players all, no wonder you've requested their repeat performance.

ANTIPASTO PLATTER

300g kalamata olives
100g slices lamb prosciutto
100g slices spicy salami

PICKLED OCTOPUS
2kg baby octopus
1 cup (250ml) water
1 clove garlic, crushed
1 medium (150g) onion,
**   finely chopped**
1 cup (250ml) white vinegar
½ cup (125ml) olive oil

PESTO SALAD
1½ cups firmly packed fresh
**   basil leaves**
1 tablespoon pine nuts, toasted
1 clove garlic, crushed
2 tablespoons grated
**   parmesan cheese**
2 tablespoons olive oil
500g bocconcini cheese, chopped
250g cherry tomatoes, halved

ROASTED CAPSICUMS
4 medium (800g) yellow capsicums
4 medium (800g) red capsicums
½ cup (125ml) olive oil
3 cloves garlic, sliced
2 tablespoons chopped
**   fresh parsley**

Just before serving, arrange olives, prosciutto, salami, pickled octopus, pesto salad and roasted capsicums on large platter.

Pickled Octopus: Remove and discard head and beak from each octopus; cut into quarters. Combine octopus pieces with water in large pan; cover, simmer about 1 hour or until octopus is tender. Drain; cool. Combine octopus with remaining ingredients in medium bowl; cover, refrigerate.

Pesto Salad: Blend or process basil, nuts, garlic, parmesan and oil until pureed. Toss bocconcini and tomatoes with pesto in medium bowl.

Roasted Capsicums: Quarter each of the capsicums, remove seeds and membranes. Roast under grill or in very hot oven, skin-side up, until skin blisters and blackens. Cover capsicum pieces in plastic or paper for 5 minutes, peel away skin; cut capsicum into 1cm strips. Toss capsicum with remaining ingredients in medium bowl.

Serves 10.

■ Pickled Octopus can be made 1 week ahead. Roasted Capsicums can be made 3 days ahead. Pesto Salad can be made a day ahead.
■ Storage: Covered, separately, in refrigerator.
■ Freeze: Not suitable.
■ Microwave: Not suitable.

FROM LEFT: Lamb Prosciutto; Kalamata Olives; Pesto Salad; Spicy Salami; Roasted Capsicums; Pickled Octopus.

PUMPKIN SOUP

20g butter
1 large (200g) onion, chopped
4 bacon rashers, chopped
1 teaspoon ground cumin
1.2kg pumpkin, peeled, chopped
1.25 litres (5 cups) chicken stock
1/2 cup (125ml) cream

Heat butter in pan; cook onion and bacon, stirring, until onion is soft. Add cumin; cook, stirring, 1 minute. Add pumpkin and stock; simmer, covered, about 25 minutes or until pumpkin is soft. Blend or process pumpkin mixture, in batches, until smooth; return to clean pan, stir over heat until heated through. Just before serving, swirl through cream.

Serves 6 to 8.

▦ Can be made 2 days ahead.
▦ Storage: Covered, in refrigerator.
▦ Freeze: Pumpkin Soup without cream suitable.
▦ Microwave: Suitable.

SPLIT GREEN PEA AND HAM SOUP

2 cups (400g) green split peas
1 medium (200g) potato, chopped
1 medium (350g) leek, chopped
1 medium (150g) onion, chopped
2.5 litres (10 cups) water
1 tablespoon olive oil
350g piece double-smoked ham, chopped
1/2 teaspoon ground cumin

Cover peas in large bowl with cold water; stand overnight.

Drain peas well; place in large pan with potato, leek, onion and water. Simmer, covered, about 2 hours or until peas are very soft; cool 10 minutes. Blend or process mixture, in batches, until smooth; strain.

Heat oil in large pan; cook ham, stirring, until browned. Add cumin; stir until fragrant. Add pea mixture to pan; simmer, uncovered, about 10 minutes or until heated through.

Serves 4 to 6.

▦ Can be made 2 days ahead.
▦ Storage: Covered, in refrigerator.
▦ Freeze: Suitable.
▦ Microwave: Not suitable.

PRAWN LAKSA

You can use 2 tablespoons of the Red Curry Paste from page 35 or one of the many commercial varieties now available in supermarkets.

100g rice vermicelli noodles
1kg medium uncooked prawns
1 tablespoon vegetable oil
2 tablespoons red curry paste
2 cloves garlic, crushed
2 teaspoons chopped fresh lemon grass
2 teaspoons ground turmeric
2 x 400ml cans coconut milk
1 litre (4 cups) water
250g asparagus, chopped
4 green onions, chopped
1 1/2 cups (120g) bean sprouts
1/4 cup chopped fresh coriander leaves
1 tablespoon lime juice
2 teaspoons fish sauce

Cover noodles in medium heatproof bowl with boiling water; allow to stand 5 minutes, drain.

Shell and devein prawns, leaving tails intact. Heat oil in large pan; cook paste, garlic, lemon grass and turmeric, stirring, until fragrant. Add coconut milk and water; bring to boil. Add noodles, prawns, asparagus and onions; simmer, uncovered, about 5 minutes or until prawns are tender. Add remaining ingredients; stir until heated through.

Serves 6.

▦ Can be made a day ahead.
▦ Storage: Covered, in refrigerator.
▦ Freeze: Not suitable.
▦ Microwave: Suitable.

Bowls from Home & Garden on the Mall; tiles from Country Floors

FROM LEFT: Prawn Laksa; Split Green Pea and Ham Soup; Pumpkin Soup.

MARINATED HONEY CHILLI CHICKEN WINGS

12 large (1.5kg) chicken wings
1/4 cup (60ml) soy sauce
2 cloves garlic, crushed
2 teaspoons grated fresh ginger
1 teaspoon sugar
2 tablespoons dry sherry
2 tablespoons peanut oil
1 tablespoon honey
2 teaspoons hot chilli sauce

1. Remove and discard tip from each wing; cut wings in half at joint.

2. Holding small end of each piece, trim around bone to cut meat free; cut, scrape and push meat towards large end. One of the 2 pieces has an extra, thinner, bone; remove and discard it.

3. Pull skin and meat down over end of bone; each wing piece will resemble a baby drumstick.

Mix chicken pieces with remaining ingredients in large bowl; cover, refrigerate 3 hours or overnight.

Heat a large wok or pan; cook undrained chicken, covered, about 15 minutes or until chicken is almost tender. Uncover, simmer, stirring occasionally, about 10 minutes or until chicken is tender and browned.

Makes 24.

■ Best prepared a day ahead.
■ Storage: Covered, in refrigerator.
■ Freeze: Marinated chicken suitable.
■ Microwave: Not suitable.

CARAMELISED CHICKEN WINGS

12 large (1.5kg) chicken wings
2 tablespoons peanut oil
3 cloves garlic, crushed
1 tablespoon chopped fresh ginger
1 tablespoon fish sauce
1 tablespoon soy sauce
1/4 cup (60ml) honey

Remove and discard tip from each wing; cut wings in half at joint. Heat oil in large wok or pan; stir-fry garlic, ginger and chicken 5 minutes. Stir in sauces and honey; cook, covered, stirring occasionally, about 15 minutes or until chicken is tender and browned.

Makes 24.

■ Best made just before serving.
■ Freeze: Not suitable.
■ Microwave: Not suitable.

BARBECUED CHICKEN WINGS

12 large (1.5kg) chicken wings
2 cloves garlic, crushed
1/4 cup (50g) firmly packed brown sugar
1/4 cup (60ml) malt vinegar
1/4 cup (60ml) Worcestershire sauce
1 cup (250ml) tomato sauce
1/2 cup (125ml) plum jam

Mix chicken with remaining ingredients in large bowl; cover, refrigerate 3 hours or overnight.

Drain chicken over bowl; reserve marinade. Place chicken on a wire rack over oven tray; brush with a little reserved marinade. Bake, uncovered, in moderately hot oven about 45 minutes or until chicken is tender and browned, brushing often with reserved marinade.

Makes 12.

■ Best prepared a day ahead.
■ Storage: Covered, in refrigerator.
■ Freeze: Not suitable.
■ Microwave: Not suitable.

OPPOSITE FROM TOP: Marinated Honey Chilli Chicken Wings; Barbecued Chicken Wings; Caramelised Chicken Wings.

Bowl and plates from The Bay Tree Kitchen shop

SPRING ROLLS WITH SWEET CHILLI SAUCE

6 dried (20g) Chinese mushrooms
500g minced pork and veal
1 medium (120g) carrot,
 coarsely grated
4 green onions, chopped
½ cup (40g) bean sprouts
3 cloves garlic, crushed
3 teaspoons grated fresh ginger
1 teaspoon sesame oil
2 teaspoons five-spice powder
2 teaspoons cornflour
2 tablespoons oyster sauce
2 tablespoons chopped fresh
 coriander leaves
30 x 25cm-square spring-
 roll wrappers
1 egg, lightly beaten
vegetable oil, for deep-frying

SWEET CHILLI DIPPING SAUCE
⅓ cup (80ml) bottled sweet
 chilli sauce
⅓ cup (80ml) water
2 teaspoons finely sliced
 fresh ginger
2 teaspoons finely chopped fresh
 coriander leaves

Cover mushrooms in small bowl with boiling water; stand 20 minutes. Drain; discard mushroom stems, slice caps.

Combine mushrooms, mince, carrot, onions, sprouts, garlic, ginger, sesame oil, five-spice, cornflour, oyster sauce and coriander in large bowl; mix well.

Spoon 1 tablespoon filling evenly across one corner of wrapper. Lightly brush edges of wrapper with a little egg; roll to enclose filling, folding in ends (spring roll should be about 11cm in length). Repeat with remaining filling and wrappers.

Deep-fry spring rolls, in batches, in hot oil until golden brown and cooked through; drain on absorbent paper. Serve with Sweet Chilli Dipping Sauce.

Sweet Chilli Dipping Sauce: Combine chilli sauce, water and ginger in small pan; simmer, uncovered, 3 minutes or until sauce thickens slightly. Just before serving, stir in coriander.

Makes 30.

■ Filling and Sweet Chilli Dipping Sauce can be prepared a day ahead. Deep-fry spring rolls just before serving.
■ Storage: Covered, separately, in refrigerator.
■ Freeze: Not suitable.
■ Microwave: Not suitable.

CHICKEN LIVER AND PORT PATE

500g chicken livers
⅓ cup (80ml) port
90g butter
1 small (80g) onion, chopped
1 clove garlic, crushed
⅓ cup (80ml) cream
¼ teaspoon ground nutmeg
½ teaspoon ground thyme
1 teaspoon gelatine
½ cup (125ml) chicken stock
4 bay leaves

Trim and wash livers; pat dry with absorbent paper. Halve livers and combine with port in small bowl; stand 2 hours. Strain livers over small bowl; reserve liquid.

Heat half the butter in medium pan; cook onion and garlic, stirring, until onion is soft. Add livers; cook, stirring, about 4 minutes or until livers change colour. Add reserved liquid; simmer, uncovered, 2 minutes. Blend or process liver mixture, cream, nutmeg and thyme until smooth; with motor operating, gradually add melted remaining butter, blend or process until smooth. Pour into 3-cup (750ml) serving dish; cover, refrigerate 2 hours.

Sprinkle gelatine over stock in cup, stand in pan of simmering water, stir until dissolved; cool. Arrange bay leaves on top of pate; carefully pour gelatine mixture over pate. Cover; refrigerate overnight.

Serves 4 to 6.

■ Can be made 2 days ahead.
■ Storage: Covered, in refrigerator.
■ Freeze: Not suitable.
■ Microwave: Butter and gelatine suitable.

Metal basket from In-House Collections; pate knife from House In Newtown

OPPOSITE: Spring Rolls with Sweet Chilli Sauce.
RIGHT: Chicken Liver and Port Pate.

SPANISH-STYLE GARLIC PRAWNS

1kg medium uncooked prawns
2 cups (500ml) olive oil
4 cloves garlic, crushed
2 small fresh red chillies, finely chopped
40g butter, chopped
2 tablespoons chopped fresh parsley

Shell and devein prawns, leaving tails intact. Divide oil, garlic and chillies among 4 x 1 cup (250ml) cast-iron dishes. Place covered dishes on oven tray in moderately hot oven about 20 minutes or until oil is bubbling.

Carefully remove dishes from oven; divide prawns among each of the 4 dishes. Cover, return to oven; bake in moderately hot oven about 10 minutes or until prawns are just tender. Divide butter and parsley among each dish; serve immediately.

Serves 4.

■ Best made just before serving.
■ Freeze: Not suitable.
■ Microwave: Not suitable.

CREAMY GARLIC PRAWNS

1kg medium uncooked prawns
60g butter
1 green onion, finely chopped
1 clove garlic, crushed
2 teaspoons plain flour
2/3 cup (160ml) chicken stock
1/4 cup (60ml) cream
1/4 cup (60ml) milk
1 tablespoon dry white wine
2 teaspoons Dijon mustard
1 teaspoon lemon juice

Shell and devein prawns, leaving tails intact. Heat butter in medium pan; cook onion and garlic, stirring, 1 minute. Add flour; cook, stirring, 1 minute. Gradually stir in combined remaining ingredients; stir over heat until sauce boils and thickens slightly. Add prawns; cook, stirring, until prawns are just tender. Serve immediately.

Serves 4.

■ Best made just before serving.
■ Freeze: Not suitable.
■ Microwave: Not suitable.

TOMATO GARLIC PRAWNS

1kg medium uncooked prawns
2 tablespoons olive oil
50g butter
1 medium (170g) red onion, chopped
3 cloves garlic, crushed
2 tablespoons dry white wine
3 large (750g) tomatoes, peeled, chopped
2 tablespoons tomato paste
1/2 teaspoon sugar
2 tablespoons chopped fresh parsley

Shell and devein prawns, leaving tails intact. Heat oil and butter in large pan; cook onion and garlic, stirring, until onion is soft. Add wine, tomatoes, paste, sugar and half the parsley; simmer, uncovered, about 5 minutes or until sauce thickens slightly. Add prawns; cook, stirring, until prawns are just tender. Serve immediately, sprinkled with remaining parsley.

Serves 4.

■ Best made just before serving.
■ Freeze: Not suitable.
■ Microwave: Not suitable.

CLOCKWISE FROM TOP RIGHT:
Spanish-Style Garlic Prawns; Creamy Garlic Prawns; Tomato Garlic Prawns.

China from Villeroy & Boch; tiles from Country Floors

Mains

The recipes you've chosen for main courses reveal a great deal about the flavour of our national identity: take several cups of English standbys, add equal parts of Mediterranean and Southeast Asian flavours then stir in a dash of Latin essence and you've created a world-class culinary selection.

SHEPHERD'S PIE

30g butter
1 medium (150g) onion, chopped
1 medium (120g) carrot,
   finely chopped
1/2 teaspoon dried mixed herbs
750g (about 4 cups) chopped
   cooked lamb
1/4 cup (60ml) tomato paste
1/4 cup (60ml) tomato sauce
2 tablespoons Worcestershire sauce
2 cups (500ml) beef stock
1 tablespoon plain flour
2 tablespoons water

POTATO TOPPING
5 medium (1kg) potatoes, chopped
60g butter, chopped
1/4 cup (60ml) milk

Oil shallow 2.5-litre (10-cup capacity) ovenproof dish.

Heat butter in large pan; cook onion and carrot, stirring, until tender. Add mixed herbs and lamb; cook, stirring, 2 minutes. Stir in paste, sauces and stock then blended flour and water; stir over heat until mixture boils and thickens. Pour mixture into prepared dish.

Spoon Potato Topping into piping bag fitted with fluted tube; pipe over lamb mixture. Bake, uncovered, in moderately hot oven about 20 minutes or until browned lightly and heated through.
Potato Topping: Boil, steam or microwave potatoes until tender; drain. Mash with butter and milk until smooth.

Serves 4.

▪ Can be made a day ahead.
▪ Storage: Covered, in refrigerator.
▪ Freeze: Suitable without topping.
▪ Microwave: Potatoes suitable.

COTTAGE PIE

2 teaspoons olive oil
1kg minced beef
2 medium (300g) onions, chopped
2 cloves garlic, crushed
2 sticks celery, chopped
1/2 teaspoon dried mixed herbs
2 cups (500ml) beef stock
1 tablespoon Worcestershire sauce
1/3 cup (80ml) tomato paste
1/4 cup (60ml) dry red wine
1/2 cup (60g) frozen peas
1 cup (125g) grated cheddar cheese

KUMARA TOPPING
600g kumara, chopped
3 medium (600g) potatoes, chopped
1/2 teaspoon ground nutmeg

Heat oil in large pan; cook mince, onions and garlic, stirring, until mince is browned. Stir in celery, herbs, stock, sauce, paste and wine; simmer, uncovered, about 30 minutes or until sauce thickens; add peas. Pour meat mixture into 2.5 litre (10-cup) ovenproof dish; spread Kumara Topping over meat mixture, sprinkle with cheese. Bake, uncovered, in moderate oven about 20 minutes or until topping is browned.
Kumara Topping: Boil, steam or microwave kumara and potatoes until tender; drain. Push mixture through a coarse sieve; stir in nutmeg.

Serves 4 to 6.

▪ Can be made a day ahead.
▪ Storage: Covered, in refrigerator.
▪ Freeze: Suitable without topping.
▪ Microwave: Kumara and potatoes suitable.

OPPOSITE FROM TOP: Cottage Pie; Shepherd's Pie.

Plates and cutlery from Villeroy & Boch; placemats from Accoutrement

TUNA SLICE

1 cup (200g) long-grain rice
50g butter
1 large (200g) onion, finely chopped
4 eggs
1 teaspoon curry powder
1½ cups (185g) grated
cheddar cheese
2 x 180g cans tuna in brine
1¼ cups (310ml) milk
1 teaspoon Dijon mustard
2 tablespoons chopped
fresh parsley

Oil 20cm x 30cm lamington pan, line base and sides with baking paper, bringing paper 3cm above edge of pan.

Cook rice in large pan of boiling water until just tender; drain, rinse under cold water, drain again. Heat the butter in small pan; cook onion, stirring, until soft.

Combine rice, half the onion, 1 egg, curry powder and a third of the cheese in large bowl; mix well then press rice mixture into prepared pan.

Strain tuna over small bowl; reserve brine. Sprinkle flaked tuna over rice mixture; top with the remaining onion mixture and cheese. Combine reserved brine, milk, mustard and parsley with remaining 3 eggs in large jug; mix well. Pour egg mixture over tuna mixture; bake, uncovered, in moderate oven about 50 minutes or until firm. Stand slice 5 minutes before cutting.

Serves 4 to 6.

■ Can be made a day ahead.
■ Storage: Covered, in refrigerator.
■ Freeze: Not suitable.
■ Microwave: Not suitable.

ZUCCHINI SLICE

2 teaspoons olive oil
1 large (200g) onion, finely chopped
4 medium (480g) zucchini,
coarsely grated
3 bacon rashers, finely chopped
1 cup (125g) grated cheddar cheese
¾ cup (105g) self-raising flour
½ cup (125ml) vegetable oil
4 eggs, lightly beaten

Oil 19cm x 29cm rectangular slice pan.

Heat oil in small pan, cook onion, stirring, until soft. Combine onion with remaining ingredients in medium bowl; mix well. Spread mixture into prepared pan; bake in moderate oven about 35 minutes or until firm.

Serves 4 to 6.

■ Can be made a day ahead.
■ Storage: Covered, in refrigerator.
■ Freeze: Not suitable.
■ Microwave: Not suitable.

BEEF AND PASTA BAKE

2 teaspoons olive oil
1 large (200g) onion, chopped
1 clove garlic, crushed
2 bacon rashers, finely chopped
1 small (70g) carrot, finely chopped
1 stick celery, finely chopped
350g button mushrooms, chopped
500g minced beef
430g can tomato soup
1/3 cup (80ml) tomato paste
1 tablespoon tomato sauce
1 teaspoon dried oregano leaves
150g spiral pasta
1 cup (125g) grated cheddar cheese

Heat oil in large pan; cook onion, garlic, bacon, carrot and celery, stirring, until carrot is just tender. Add mushrooms; cook, stirring, 2 minutes. Add mince; cook, stirring until mince just changes colour. Add undiluted soup, paste, sauce and oregano; simmer, covered, about 15 minutes or until mixture has thickened slightly.

Meanwhile, cook pasta in large pan of boiling water until just tender; drain. Stir pasta into mince mixture; spoon mixture into oiled deep 2-litre (8-cup) ovenproof dish then sprinkle over top with grated cheese. Bake, uncovered, in moderate oven about 15 minutes or until browned lightly.

Serves 6.
- Can be made a day ahead.
- Storage: Covered, in refrigerator.
- Freeze: Suitable.
- Microwave: Not suitable.

OPPOSITE FROM TOP: Zucchini Slice; Tuna Slice.
ABOVE: Beef and Pasta Bake.

MONGOLIAN LAMB

1kg lamb strips
1 teaspoon five-spice powder
2 teaspoons sugar
1 tablespoon cornflour
1/3 cup (80ml) light soy sauce
1 tablespoon black bean sauce
3 cloves garlic, crushed
1 1/2 tablespoons rice wine vinegar
1 egg, lightly beaten
1/4 cup (60ml) peanut oil
3 medium (450g) onions, sliced
1/3 cup (80ml) beef stock
1/4 teaspoon sesame oil
2 green onions, finely sliced

Combine lamb, spice, sugar, cornflour, half the sauces, garlic, vinegar and egg in medium bowl; mix well. Cover, refrigerate 1 hour. Drain lamb over small bowl; reserve marinade.

Heat half the peanut oil in wok or large pan; stir-fry lamb, in batches, until tender. Remove lamb from wok.

Heat remaining oil in wok; stir-fry onions until soft. Return lamb to wok with reserved marinade, remaining half of sauces, stock and sesame oil; stir until mixture boils and thickens. Serve sprinkled with green onions.

Serves 4 to 6.

■ Best made just before serving.
■ Freeze: Not suitable.
■ Microwave: Not suitable.

MARINATED LAMB CUTLETS WITH KUMARA PUREE

16 (800g) lamb cutlets
1/2 cup (125ml) olive oil
1/4 cup (60ml) lemon juice
2 tablespoons balsamic vinegar
4 cloves garlic, crushed
2 tablespoons honey
**1 tablespoon chopped
  fresh rosemary**

KUMARA PUREE
2 medium (800g) kumara, chopped
2/3 cup (160ml) buttermilk
20g butter
1 teaspoon chicken stock powder
1 clove garlic, crushed
1 teaspoon chopped fresh rosemary

Combine cutlets with oil, juice, vinegar, garlic, honey and rosemary in large dish. Cover; refrigerate 3 hours or overnight.

Drain cutlets from marinade; discard marinade. Grill or barbecue cutlets, in batches, on both sides until cooked as desired. Serve with Kumara Puree.

Kumara Puree: Boil, steam or microwave kumara until tender; drain. Mash kumara with remaining ingredients until smooth.

Serves 6 to 8.

■ Lamb Cutlets best prepared a day ahead. Kumara Puree can be made a day ahead.
■ Storage: Covered, separately, in refrigerator.
■ Freeze: Not suitable.
■ Microwave: Kumara suitable.

OPPOSITE : Mongolian Lamb.
BELOW: Marinated Lamb Cutlets with Kumara Puree.

TOMATO MARINARA PASTA

We used spaghetti here but you can use the pasta of your choice.

500g medium uncooked prawns
500g marinara seafood mix
1 tablespoon olive oil
1 medium (150g) onion, chopped
2 cloves garlic, crushed
5 large (1.25kg) tomatoes, peeled, chopped
1/3 cup (80ml) dry white wine
1/2 cup (125ml) water
2 tablespoons tomato paste
500g pasta
1 tablespoon chopped fresh parsley

Peel and devein prawns, leaving tails intact. Rinse marinara mix under cold water; drain well.

Heat oil in large pan; cook onion and garlic, stirring, until onion is soft. Add tomatoes, wine, water and paste; simmer, uncovered, about 15 minutes or until sauce thickens.

Add prawns and marinara mix; simmer, uncovered, about 5 minutes or until seafood is tender.

Meanwhile, cook pasta in large pan of boiling water, uncovered, until just tender; drain. Stir parsley into marinara sauce; serve over hot pasta.

Serves 4.

■ Best made just before serving.
■ Freeze: Sauce, without seafood, suitable.
■ Microwave: Not suitable.

CREAMY MARINARA PASTA

We used spinach fettuccine here but you can use the pasta of your choice.

500g medium uncooked prawns
500g marinara seafood mix
30g butter
1 small (80g) onion, chopped
2 cloves garlic, crushed
1 tablespoon plain flour
1/4 cup (60ml) dry white wine
1 cup (250ml) cream
1/2 cup (125ml) water
500g pasta
1 tablespoon chopped fresh parsley

Shell and devein prawns, leaving tails intact. Rinse marinara mix under cold water; drain well.

Heat butter in large pan; cook onion and garlic, stirring, until onion is soft. Stir in flour until mixture is dry and grainy. Gradually stir in combined wine, cream and water; stir over heat until mixture boils and thickens. Add seafood; simmer, uncovered, about 5 minutes or until seafood is tender.

Meanwhile, cook pasta in large pan of boiling water, uncovered, until just tender; drain. Stir parsley into marinara sauce; serve over hot pasta.

Serves 4.

■ Best made just before serving.
■ Freeze: Not suitable.
■ Microwave: Not suitable.

White china from Villeroy & Boch

Platter from Kitchen Kapers; powder bowl from Wedg Unique

LEFT FROM TOP: *Creamy Marinara Pasta;
Tomato Marinara Pasta.*
OPPOSITE: *Roast Sirloin of Beef with
Horseradish Seasoning.*

ROAST SIRLOIN OF BEEF WITH HORSERADISH SEASONING

2.5kg boneless sirloin roast
1½ cups (375ml) water
½ cup (125ml) cream
1 tablespoon cornflour
1 tablespoon brandy
2 tablespoons port
1 teaspoon Dijon mustard
1 beef stock cube

SEASONING
90g butter
2 bacon rashers, chopped
1 medium (150g) onion, chopped
1½ tablespoons horseradish relish
2 tablespoons chopped
    fresh parsley
1 egg
2 cups (140g) stale breadcrumbs

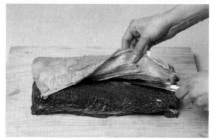

Cut between fat and meat of roast to make a pocket for seasoning; trim off and discard a little of the fat. Spoon seasoning into pocket; tie roast with string at 3cm intervals.

Place roast, fat side up, in flameproof baking dish. Bake, uncovered, in hot oven for 20 minutes; reduce heat to moderate, bake about 45 minutes or

until cooked as desired. Remove roast from dish; stand, covered, 10 minutes.

Drain and discard all but 2 table-spoons of fat from dish. Add water, cream and blended remaining ingredients to dish. Cook, stirring, until sauce boils and thickens slightly; strain.

Seasoning: Melt butter in small pan, add bacon and onion; cook, stirring, until onion is soft. Cool. Combine bacon mixture with remaining ingredients in medium bowl; mix well.

Serves 6 to 8.

■ Best made just before serving.
■ Freeze: Not suitable.
■ Microwave: Not suitable.

BASIC PIZZA DOUGH

This recipe makes enough dough for a 30cm-round pizza.

2 teaspoons (7g) dried yeast
½ teaspoon sugar
¾ cup (180ml) warm water
2 cups (300g) plain flour
1 teaspoon salt
2 tablespoons olive oil

Combine yeast, sugar and water in small bowl; cover, stand in warm place 10 minutes. Sift flour and salt into large bowl; stir in yeast mixture and oil, mix to a soft dough. Turn dough onto floured surface; knead about 5 minutes or until smooth and elastic. Place dough in oiled bowl; cover, stand in a warm place about 1 hour or until dough is doubled in size.

Knead dough on floured surface until smooth, roll out as directed in recipes or to fit pizza tray.

■ Best made just before baking.
■ Freeze: Not suitable.
■ Microwave: Not suitable.

BASIC TOMATO SAUCE

This recipe makes enough sauce for a 30cm-round pizza.

1 tablespoon olive oil
1 small (80g) onion, finely chopped
2 cloves garlic, crushed
400g can tomatoes
¼ cup (60ml) tomato paste
1 teaspoon sugar
1 tablespoon chopped
   fresh oregano

Heat oil in medium pan; cook onion and garlic, stirring, until onion is soft. Add undrained crushed tomatoes and the remaining ingredients; simmer, uncovered, about 15 minutes or until mixture has thickened.

■ Can be made 2 days ahead.
■ Storage: Covered, in refrigerator.
■ Freeze: Suitable.
■ Microwave: Not suitable.

THE DELI-DELIGHT PIZZA

1 large (350g) red capsicum
100g sliced pancetta
1 quantity Basic Pizza Dough
1 quantity Basic Tomato Sauce
4 drained marinated
   artichokes, sliced
½ cup (75g) sliced sun-dried
   tomatoes in oil, drained
⅓ cup (50g) pimiento-stuffed green
   olives, halved
2 tablespoons pine nuts
¾ cup (75g) grated
   mozzarella cheese
¼ cup fresh basil leaves

Quarter capsicum, remove seeds and membranes. Roast under grill or in very hot oven, skin-side up, until skin blisters and blackens. Cover capsicum pieces in plastic or paper for 5 minutes, peel away skin; cut capsicum into thin strips. Cut pancetta into thin strips.

Roll Basic Pizza Dough on a floured surface to form a 30cm round; place on oiled pizza tray or oven tray. Spread with Basic Tomato Sauce then sprinkle capsicum, pancetta, artichokes, tomatoes, olives, pine nuts and cheese. Bake in hot oven about 35 minutes or until browned. Sprinkle pizza with basil.

Serves 4.

■ Best made just before serving.
■ Freeze: Suitable.
■ Microwave: Not suitable.

MUSHROOM PIZZA

300g button mushrooms,
   thinly sliced
2 cloves garlic, crushed
2 tablespoons chopped fresh mint
1 tablespoon olive oil
1 quantity Basic Pizza Dough
1 quantity Basic Tomato Sauce
¼ cup (25g) grated
   mozzarella cheese
¼ cup (30g) grated tasty
   cheddar cheese

Combine mushrooms, garlic, mint and oil in medium bowl. Roll Basic Pizza Dough on a floured surface to form a 30cm round; place on oiled pizza tray or oven tray. Spread with Basic Tomato Sauce then sprinkle with combined cheeses; top with mushroom mixture. Bake in hot oven about 35 minutes or until browned.

Serves 4.

■ Best made just before serving.
■ Freeze: Suitable.
■ Microwave: Not suitable.

SPINACH, BACON AND FETTA PIZZA

1 bunch (500g) English spinach,
   roughly chopped
1 quantity Basic Pizza Dough
1 teaspoon sambal oelek
1 quantity Basic Tomato Sauce
4 bacon rashers, chopped
200g fetta cheese, crumbled
2 tablespoons finely grated
   parmesan cheese

Boil, steam or microwave spinach until wilted; drain. Squeeze out excess moisture from spinach.

Roll Basic Pizza Dough on a floured surface to form a 30cm round; place on oiled pizza tray or oven tray. Stir sambal oelek into Basic Tomato Sauce; spread onto pizza base then sprinkle spinach and remaining ingredients over sauce. Bake in hot oven about 35 minutes or until browned.

Serves 4.

■ Best made just before serving.
■ Freeze: Suitable.
■ Microwave: Not suitable.

OPPOSITE FROM TOP: Spinach, Bacon and Fetta Pizza; Mushroom Pizza; The Deli-Delight Pizza.

SAVOURY IMPOSSIBLE PIE

1/3 cup (50g) plain flour
1 1/2 cups (375ml) milk
3 eggs
2 bacon rashers, chopped
3 green onions, chopped
1 cup (125g) grated cheddar cheese
130g can corn kernels,
   rinsed, drained
2 tablespoons chopped
   fresh parsley

Oil shallow 23cm-round flan dish. Whisk flour and milk in medium bowl until smooth; whisk in eggs. Stir in remaining ingredients; pour mixture into prepared dish. Bake in moderately slow oven about 1 hour or until set.

Serves 4 to 6.

■ Best made just before serving.
■ Freeze: Not suitable.
■ Microwave: Not suitable.

ABOVE: Savoury Impossible Pie.
OPPOSITE IN BOWLS: Chilli Plum Glaze, left; Honey Mustard Glaze, right.

GLAZED BEEF AND PORK SPARE RIBS

Both of the glaze recipes here can be used with 2kg of any one of the following rib varieties: American-style pork spare ribs; pork-belly ribs; American-style beef spare ribs; full-backed beef ribs; individual beef ribs.

HONEY MUSTARD GLAZE
½ cup (125ml) orange juice
½ cup (125ml) honey
½ cup (125ml) barbecue sauce
2 tablespoons soy sauce
1 tablespoon seeded mustard
3 cloves garlic, crushed

CHILLI PLUM GLAZE
⅓ cup (80ml) plum sauce
⅓ cup (80ml) tomato sauce
⅓ cup (65g) firmly packed
  brown sugar
¼ cup (60ml) chilli sauce
¼ cup (60ml) Worcestershire sauce
¼ cup (60ml) cider vinegar
1 tablespoon grated fresh ginger
2 fresh red chillies, sliced

Place preferred type of rib on wire rack over large baking dish; brush all over with preferred glaze. Barbecue (or bake, uncovered, in moderate oven) about 1 to 1¼ hours or until browned and tender. Brush ribs with glaze and turn occasionally during cooking.

Honey Mustard Glaze: Combine all ingredients in large jug; mix well. Makes about 1¾ cups (430ml).
Chilli Plum Glaze: Combine all the ingredients in large jug; mix well. Makes about 1¾ cups (430ml).

Each recipe serves 4 to 6.

■ Glazes can be made a day ahead.
■ Storage: Covered, in refrigerator.
■ Freeze: Not suitable.
■ Microwave: Not suitable.

Small bowls and brushes from The Bay Tree Kitchen Shop

LOUISE'S VEGETARIAN LASAGNE

3 medium (900g) eggplants
salt
1/4 cup (60ml) olive oil
4 medium (800g) red capsicums
750g jar Paul Newman's Own
 Venetian-Style Spaghetti Sauce
250g packet instant lasagne
 pasta sheets
250g mozzarella cheese,
 thinly sliced

PISTACHIO PESTO
1/2 cup (75g) shelled pistachios
1 cup firmly packed fresh
 basil leaves
1/3 cup (80ml) olive oil
2 cloves garlic, crushed
2 tablespoons grated
 parmesan cheese

WHITE SAUCE
80g butter
1/3 cup (50g) plain flour
2 1/2 cups (625ml) milk
1/2 cup (40g) grated
 parmesan cheese

Oil a 6cm-deep rectangular 3.5-litre (14-cup) ovenproof dish. Cut eggplants into 1cm slices, sprinkle all over with salt; stand 20 minutes.

Rinse eggplant slices under cold water; drain, pat dry with absorbent paper. Brush eggplant with oil; place in single layer on 2 oven trays. Bake eggplant in moderately hot oven about 40 minutes or until browned and tender.

Quarter capsicums, remove seeds and membranes. Roast under grill or in a very hot oven, skin-side up, until skin blisters and blackens. Cover capsicum pieces in plastic or paper for 5 minutes, peel away skin; cut capsicum into thick strips.

Spread a third of the spaghetti sauce into prepared dish. Top with a third of the lasagne sheets, another third of the spaghetti sauce, half the eggplant, half the cheese, another third of the lasagne sheets, then remaining spaghetti sauce, capsicum, cheese, lasagne sheets and eggplant. Spread Pistachio Pesto over eggplant; top with White Sauce. Bake, covered, in moderate oven 30 minutes,

then uncover, bake about 30 minutes or until browned. Stand for 5 minutes before serving.

Pistachio Pesto: Blend or process all ingredients until pureed.

White Sauce: Melt butter in medium pan; add flour, stir over heat until bubbling and grainy. Remove from heat, gradually stir in milk; stir over heat until mixture boils and thickens. Remove from heat, stir in cheese.

Serves 6 to 8.

■ Can be made a day ahead.
■ Storage: Covered, in refrigerator.
■ Freeze: Suitable.
■ Microwave: White sauce suitable.

SATAY CHICKEN SKEWERS

Before using skewers, soak them in cold water for several hours to stop them from scorching when satays are cooking.

12 (1.3kg) chicken thigh fillets
1 cup (250ml) chicken stock
1/2 cup (130g) crunchy peanut butter
1/4 cup (60ml) mild sweet
   chilli sauce
1 tablespoon lime juice
1/4 cup (60ml) coconut milk
2 teaspoons brown sugar

Cut each fillet into 12 cubes; thread on 12 skewers. Cook skewers, in batches, in heated oiled griddle pan (or grill or barbecue) until tender.

Combine remaining ingredients in medium pan; stir over heat about 5 minutes or until sauce thickens. Serve sauce over chicken skewers.

Serves 4 to 6.

■ Best made just before serving.
■ Freeze: Not suitable.
■ Microwave: Not suitable.

OPPOSITE: Louise's Vegetarian Lasagne.
ABOVE: Satay Chicken Skewers.

BEEF BURRITOS

4 x 25cm-round flour tortillas
1 cup (125g) grated cheddar cheese
1 teaspoon hot paprika
3/4 cup (180ml) sour cream
1 tablespoon chopped fresh
coriander leaves

BEAN AND BEEF FILLING
1 tablespoon olive oil
500g minced beef
1 medium (150g) onion,
finely chopped
1 clove garlic, crushed
425g can tomatoes
35g packet taco seasoning mix
1/2 cup (125ml) water
300g can kidney beans,
rinsed, drained

GUACAMOLE
1 large (320g) avocado
1 small (80g) onion, finely chopped
2 teaspoons lime or lemon juice
few drops Tabasco sauce
1 small (130g) tomato, seeded,
finely chopped

Divide warm Bean and Beef Filling among the tortillas, roll; secure with toothpicks. Place filled tortillas on oiled oven tray; sprinkle with cheese and paprika. Bake in moderately hot oven about 10 minutes or until heated through. Remove toothpicks; serve topped with guacamole, sour cream and fresh coriander leaves.

Bean and Beef Filling: Heat oil in medium pan; cook beef, stirring, until browned. Add onion and garlic; cook, stirring, until onion is soft. Stir in undrained crushed tomatoes and remaining ingredients; simmer, uncovered, about 15 minutes or until mixture is thickened.

Guacamole: Mash avocado in medium bowl with fork; add remaining ingredients, mix well.

Serves 4.

■ Must be made just before serving. Beef and Bean Filling can be made a day ahead.
■ Storage: Covered, in refrigerator.
■ Freeze: Not suitable.
■ Microwave: Not suitable.

NACHOS

A 460g can of borlotti beans can be substituted for the minced beef.

1 tablespoon olive oil
1 medium (150g) onion, chopped
2 cloves garlic, crushed
500g minced beef
1 tablespoon ground cumin
1 teaspoon hot paprika
400g can tomatoes
2 medium (500g) avocados, chopped
2 teaspoons lemon juice
few drops Tabasco sauce
230g packet corn chips
1 1/4 cups (155g) grated
cheddar cheese
1 medium (190g) tomato,
seeded, chopped
3/4 cup (180ml) sour cream

Heat oil in pan; cook onion and garlic, stirring, until onion is soft. Add mince; cook, stirring, until mince is browned. Add spices; cook, stirring, until fragrant. Add undrained crushed tomatoes; cook, uncovered, about 15 minutes or until most of the liquid has evaporated.

Mash avocados in medium bowl with a fork; add lemon juice and Tabasco to taste, mash until combined.

Spread corn chips in a shallow oven-proof serving dish; top with cheese. Bake in moderately hot oven until cheese is melted and just browned; top with mince mixture, avocado mixture, tomato and sour cream.

Serves 4 as entree or 2 as a main meal.

■ Must be made just before serving. Mince mixture can be made a day ahead.
■ Storage: Covered, in refrigerator.
■ Freeze: Not suitable.
■ Microwave: Not suitable.

Plate from The Bay Tree Kitchen Shop

OPPOSITE FROM TOP: Nachos; Beef Burritos.

CHICKEN ELIZABETH

1 litre (4 cups) water
½ cup (125ml) dry white wine
2 bay leaves
6 peppercorns
2 fresh stalks parsley
6 single (1kg) chicken breast fillets

MANGO MAYONNAISE
1 cup (250ml) mayonnaise
1 tablespoon lemon juice
2 teaspoons curry powder
⅓ cup (80ml) mango chutney
2 tablespoons chopped fresh mint

Combine water, wine, leaves, peppercorns and parsley in large pan; bring to boil. Add chicken; cover, simmer about 10 minutes or until tender. Remove chicken, pat dry with absorbent paper; cover, refrigerate until cold. Serve chicken with Mango Mayonnaise.
Mango Mayonnaise: Combine all ingredients in small bowl; mix well.

Serves 6.

◼ Can be prepared a day ahead.
◼ Storage: Covered, separately, in refrigerator.
◼ Freeze: Not suitable.
◼ Microwave: Chicken suitable.

APRICOT CHICKEN

1.5kg chicken drumsticks
35g packet salt-reduced French onion soup mix
425ml can apricot nectar

Remove and discard skin from chicken.
Combine chicken, dry soup mix and nectar in medium baking dish. Cover, bake in moderate oven 40 minutes, then uncover, bake about 30 minutes or until chicken is brown and tender.

Serves 4.

◼ Best made just before serving.
◼ Freeze: Not suitable.
◼ Microwave: Not suitable.

LEMON CHICKEN

1.5kg chicken pieces
1 litre (4 cups) water
3 egg yolks, lightly beaten
½ cup (75g) rice flour
vegetable oil, for deep-frying

LEMON SAUCE
⅓ cup (50g) cornflour
⅓ cup (75g) sugar
½ cup (125ml) lemon juice
2 tablespoons lemon butter
1 teaspoon grated fresh ginger
1 teaspoon dry sherry

Using a cleaver, chop wings, breast halves, legs and thighs into about 3 pieces each. Bring water to boil in large pan, add chicken pieces; simmer, covered, about 10 minutes or until chicken is just cooked. Drain chicken over large bowl; reserve 2½ cups of the stock.
Dip each chicken piece in egg yolk then in flour, shake off excess. Deep-fry chicken, in batches, in hot oil until brown and crisp; drain on absorbent paper. Serve chicken with Lemon Sauce.
Lemon Sauce: Blend cornflour and sugar with a little of the reserved stock in a medium pan; gradually stir in the remaining stock then remaining ingredients. Stir over heat until sauce boils and thickens.

Serves 4.

◼ Chicken can be prepared 3 hours ahead and deep-fried just before serving. Lemon Sauce can be made a day ahead.
◼ Storage: Covered, separately, in refrigerator.
◼ Freeze: Not suitable.
◼ Microwave: Not suitable.

Pewter platter, glasses and napkins from Home & Garden on the Mall; plates and jug from Corso De' Fiori

CLOCKWISE FROM TOP: Chicken Elizabeth; Apricot Chicken; Lemon Chicken.

SUPREME COTTAGE LOAF

23cm-round cottage bread loaf
2 large (700g) red capsicums
2 large (1kg) eggplants
salt
2 medium (800g) kumaras
3 medium (360g) zucchini
1/2 cup (125ml) olive oil
1/3 cup firmly packed fresh
    basil leaves
3/4 cup (150g) ricotta cheese
1/4 cup (20g) grated
    parmesan cheese

SUN-DRIED TOMATO PUREE
1 cup (150g) sun-dried tomatoes
    in oil, drained
2 cloves garlic, crushed
1/4 cup lightly packed fresh
    oregano leaves
1 tablespoon seeded mustard
1/4 cup (60ml) olive oil

Cut lid from top of loaf, remove soft bread inside loaf, leaving 2cm shell. Brush Sun-Dried Tomato Puree inside lid and bread shell. Quarter capsicums, remove seeds and membranes. Roast under grill or in very hot oven, skin-side up, until skin blisters and blackens. Cover capsicum pieces in plastic or paper for 5 minutes, peel away skin.

Cut eggplants into 1.5cm slices, sprinkle all over with salt; stand 30 minutes. Rinse eggplant under cold water; drain on absorbent paper. Cut kumaras and zucchini into 5mm slices. Brush eggplant, kumara and zucchini slices with oil; grill, in batches, until lightly browned; drain on absorbent paper.

Place kumara inside bread shell; top with basil leaves, capsicum, zucchini, combined cheeses and eggplant. Replace lid, wrap loaf completely in plastic wrap, place on oven tray, top with another oven tray, weight with brick; refrigerate overnight.

Remove and discard plastic wrap; place loaf on oven tray. Bake in very hot oven about 5 minutes or until crisp.
Sun-Dried Tomato Puree: Blend or process tomatoes, garlic, oregano and mustard until almost smooth. Add oil gradually, in a thin steam, with motor operating, until combined.

Serves 8 to 10.

■ Must be made a day ahead.
■ Storage: Covered, in refrigerator.
■ Freeze: Not suitable.
■ Microwave: Not suitable.

FETTUCCINE CARBONARA

500g fettuccine pasta
6 bacon rashers, thinly sliced
300ml cream
4 eggs, lightly beaten
1 cup (80g) grated
    parmesan cheese

Cook pasta in large pan of boiling water, uncovered, until just tender. Drain, keep warm while making sauce.

Cook bacon in medium pan, stirring, until crisp. Add cream; stir until heated through. Working quickly, gently mix bacon mixture with hot pasta and combined eggs and cheese in large bowl.

Serves 4.
■ Must be made just before serving.
■ Freeze: Not suitable.
■ Microwave: Not suitable.

Basket from Kitchen Kapers

LEFT: Supreme Cottage Loaf.
OPPOSITE: Fettuccine Carbonara.

RICH GLAZED MEATLOAF

500g minced beef
250g sausage mince
1 egg, lightly beaten
1 small (80g) onion, chopped
1 stick celery, chopped
1 small (70g) carrot, grated
1 tablespoon chopped fresh parsley
1 tablespoon tomato sauce
2 teaspoons Worcestershire sauce
2 teaspoons Dijon mustard
1 cup (70g) stale breadcrumbs

GLAZE
½ cup (125ml) water
½ cup (125ml) tomato sauce
¼ cup (60ml) Worcestershire sauce
2 tablespoons malt vinegar
**¼ cup (50g) firmly packed
   brown sugar**
1 teaspoon instant coffee powder
30g butter
2 tablespoons lemon juice

Combine all ingredients in large bowl; mix well. Flatten meatloaf mixture on large sheet baking paper to form 25cm x 35cm rectangle; roll as for a Swiss roll, from short side, using paper as a guide. Place in baking dish, seam-side down. Bake, uncovered, in moderate oven 30 minutes; remove from oven, pour off and discard excess fat. Pour glaze over meatloaf; bake, uncovered, about 30 minutes or until firm and cooked through, brushing occasionally with glaze.

Glaze: Combine all ingredients in small pan; bring to boil then simmer immediately, uncovered, 5 minutes.

Serves 6.

- Meatloaf and Glaze can be prepared a day ahead.
- Storage: Covered, separately, in refrigerator.
- Freeze: Meatloaf suitable.
- Microwave: Not suitable.

GREEN CHICKEN CURRY

750g chicken thigh fillets
200g green beans, chopped
1 cup (250ml) coconut cream

GREEN CURRY PASTE
3 small fresh green chillies, chopped
3 green onions, chopped
2 cloves garlic, crushed
¼ cup chopped fresh lemon grass
**¼ cup chopped fresh
   coriander leaves**
2 tablespoons peanut oil
2 tablespoons water
1 teaspoon shrimp paste
½ teaspoon ground cumin
¼ teaspoon ground turmeric

Cut chicken into thin strips. Cook Green Curry Paste in a heated dry pan, stirring, about 3 minutes or until fragrant. Add chicken and beans; cook, stirring, about 5 minutes or until chicken is just tender. Stir in coconut cream; simmer, uncovered, about 3 minutes or until sauce is thickened.

Green Curry Paste: Blend or process all ingredients until smooth.

Serves 6.

■ Green Curry Paste can be made a week ahead. Green Chicken Curry best made just before serving.

▩ Storage: Curry Paste, in airtight container, in refrigerator.

▩ Freeze: Not suitable.

▩ Microwave: Suitable.

RED CHICKEN CURRY

2 tablespoons peanut oil
4 green onions, chopped
750g chicken thigh fillets, chopped
2 tablespoons fish sauce
1 cup (250ml) coconut milk

RED CURRY PASTE
1 small (100g) red onion, chopped
3 cloves garlic, crushed
2 tablespoons chopped fresh lemon grass
3 teaspoons chopped fresh coriander roots
2 teaspoons dried chilli flakes
1 teaspoon galangal powder
1 teaspoon grated lime rind
½ teaspoon shrimp paste
1 dried kaffir lime leaf
3 teaspoons sweet paprika
½ teaspoon ground turmeric
½ teaspoon cumin seeds
3 teaspoons peanut oil

Heat oil in wok or large pan; cook ⅓ cup Red Curry Paste and green onions, stirring, for about 2 minutes or until fragrant. Reserve remaining Red Curry Paste for another use.

Add chicken; stir-fry about 5 minutes or until chicken is just tender. Stir in fish sauce and coconut milk; bring to boil then immediately simmer, uncovered, until mixture is heated through.

Red Curry Paste: Blend or process all ingredients until smooth.

Serves 6.

■ Red Curry Paste can be made a week ahead. Red Chicken Curry can be made a day ahead.

▩ Storage: Curry Paste, in airtight container, in refrigerator. Chicken Curry, covered, in refrigerator.

▩ Freeze: Suitable.

▩ Microwave: Not suitable.

OPPOSITE: Rich Glazed Meatloaf.
RIGHT FROM TOP: Red Chicken Curry; Green Chicken Curry.

China from Villeroy & Boch; tray from Accoutrement

Vegetables & Salads

Not so much accompaniments as stars in their own right, these salad and potato recipes are a few of those beguiling dishes that have recently become established as new "traditional" favourites: potato skins and the Caesar salad have taken that culinary step forward from restaurant menu to the dinner table... and our hearts.

CAJUN POTATO WEDGES WITH SWEET CHILLI SAUCE

8 medium (1.6kg) potatoes
¼ cup (60ml) olive oil
90g butter, melted
2 tablespoons Cajun seasoning
2 tablespoons ground cumin

SWEET CHILLI DIPPING SAUCE
⅓ cup (80ml) mild sweet
chilli sauce
300ml sour cream

Halve unpeeled potatoes; cut each half into 4 wedges. Boil, steam or microwave potatoes until just tender; drain, cool.

Combine oil, butter and spices in large bowl; add potatoes, mix gently to coat well. Place wedges, in single layer, on oven trays; bake, uncovered, in hot oven about 45 minutes or until crisp. Serve with Sweet Chilli Dipping Sauce.
Sweet Chilli Dipping Sauce: Combine ingredients in bowl; mix well.

Makes 64.
▒ Best made just before serving. Sweet Chilli Dipping Sauce can be made a day ahead.
▒ Storage: Sauce, covered, in refrigerator.
▒ Freeze: Not suitable.
▒ Microwave: Potatoes suitable.

PARMESAN POTATOES

10 large (3kg) potatoes
60g butter, melted
⅔ cup (50g) grated
parmesan cheese

Halve peeled potatoes. Place, cut-side down, on board; slice into potatoes at 3mm intervals, being careful not to cut all the way through base.

Place potatoes, base-down, in oiled baking dish; brush all over with butter. Bake, uncovered, in moderate oven for 40 minutes, brushing occasionally. Sprinkle with parmesan; bake, uncovered, in moderately hot oven about 40 minutes or until potatoes are crisp outside and tender inside. Do not turn potatoes during cooking.

Serves 6 to 8.
▒ Can be prepared 2 hours ahead.
▒ Storage: Covered, in refrigerator.
▒ Freeze: Not suitable.
▒ Microwave: Not suitable.

POTATO SKINS

5 medium (1kg) potatoes
2 tablespoons olive oil
½ teaspoon fine sea salt
1 teaspoon cracked black pepper
300ml sour cream

Scrub potatoes, dry thoroughly; brush all over with half the oil, place on oven tray. Bake, uncovered, in hot oven about 1 hour or until tender; cool.

Cut each potato into 6 wedges; scoop out flesh carefully, leaving skins intact (reserve potato flesh for another use). Place potato skins, outsides up, in single layer on wire rack over oven tray; brush with remaining oil, sprinkle with combined sea salt and cracked pepper. Bake, uncovered, in hot oven about 30 minutes or until crisp; serve with sour cream, if desired.

Makes 30.
▒ Whole potatoes can be baked a day ahead. Potato Skins best made just before serving.
▒ Storage: Covered, in refrigerator.
▒ Freeze: Not suitable.
▒ Microwave: Whole potatoes suitable.

OPPOSITE FROM TOP: Parmesan Potatoes; Potato Skins; Cajun Potato Wedges with Sweet Chilli Sauce.

LAYERED GARDEN SALAD

½ iceberg lettuce, shredded
2 cups (250g) frozen peas, thawed
2 hard-boiled eggs
250g button mushrooms,
   finely sliced
1 cup (125g) grated tasty
   cheddar cheese
1 cup (250ml) mayonnaise
2 tablespoons sour cream
2 teaspoons Dijon mustard
1 tablespoon lemon juice
6 green onions, finely chopped
4 bacon rashers, finely chopped
1 large (250g) tomato, sliced
2 tablespoons chopped
   fresh parsley

Place lettuce in deep 3.5-litre (14-cup) dish; cover lettuce evenly with peas. Push eggs through sieve into small bowl; stir in mushrooms then spoon over peas, top with cheese. Combine mayonnaise, cream, mustard, juice and onions in small bowl, pour over cheese. Cover; refrigerate 1 hour.

Cook bacon in small heated pan, stirring, until crisp and browned; drain on absorbent paper. Arrange tomato slices over mayonnaise layer; sprinkle with bacon and parsley.

Serves 6 to 8.

▨ Best made a day ahead.
▨ Storage: Covered, in refrigerator.
▨ Freeze: Not suitable.
▨ Microwave: Bacon suitable.

Bowl and servers from Kitchen Kapers

CREAMY POTATO, CHEESE AND BACON BAKE

Do not use thickened cream for this recipe. We used cheddar cheese here but Swiss cheese is equally good.

4 bacon rashers, chopped
4 large (1.2kg) potatoes
1 cup (125g) grated tasty
   cheddar cheese
300ml pouring cream
20g butter, chopped

Cook bacon in small heated pan; stir until lightly browned and just crisp.

Peel potatoes; slice thinly. Layer potatoes with bacon and cheese in a 2-litre (8-cup) ovenproof dish; pour over cream, dot with butter. Bake, covered, in moderately hot oven 40 minutes; uncover, bake about 35 minutes or until top is browned and potatoes are tender.

Serves 4 to 6.

▨ Can be made a day ahead.
▨ Storage: Covered, in refrigerator.
▨ Freeze: Not suitable.
▨ Microwave: Bacon suitable.

ABOVE: Layered Garden Salad.
BELOW: Creamy Potato, Cheese and Bacon Bake.
OPPOSITE: Best Caesar Salad.

BEST CAESAR SALAD

6 bacon rashers, chopped
6 slices white bread
2 tablespoons olive oil
1 medium cos lettuce
5 (about 25g) anchovy fillets,
   finely sliced
3/4 cup (60g) flaked
   parmesan cheese

CAESAR DRESSING
1 egg
1 clove garlic, crushed
2 tablespoons lemon juice
1 teaspoon Dijon mustard
1/4 cup (20g) grated
   parmesan cheese
5 (about 25g) anchovy fillets
3/4 cup (180ml) olive oil

Cook bacon in small heated pan until crisp; drain on absorbent paper.

Remove crusts from bread, cut into 5cm shapes; brush both sides each shape with oil, place on oven tray. Bake, uncovered, turning occasionally, in moderate oven about 10 minutes or until croutons are lightly browned; cool.

Combine torn lettuce leaves in large bowl with half of each of the bacon, croutons, anchovy slices and flaked cheese; pour over half the Caesar Dressing, mix well. Top with remaining bacon, croutons, anchovy slices, flaked cheese and Caesar Dressing.

Caesar Dressing: Blend or process egg, garlic, juice, mustard, cheese and anchovies until smooth. Add oil, in a thin stream, while motor is operating; blend or process until thick.

Serves 4.

■ Croutons and Caesar Dressing can be made a day ahead.
■ Storage: Croutons, in air-tight container. Dressing, covered, in refrigerator.
■ Freeze: Not suitable.
■ Microwave: Bacon suitable.

Microwave Favourites

GINGER CREAM PUMPKIN

This recipe was tested in a 700-watt microwave oven.

1kg butternut pumpkin
½ cup (125ml) milk
½ cup (125ml) cream
½ teaspoon grated fresh ginger
½ teaspoon grated orange rind
½ cup (60g) grated cheddar cheese
1 tablespoon chopped fresh chives
2 teaspoons cornflour
2 teaspoons water

Peel, seed and slice pumpkin, place in shallow microwave-safe dish; cover. Microwave on HIGH (100%) about 10 minutes or until tender.

Combine milk, cream, ginger, rind, cheese, chives and blended cornflour and water in microwave-safe jug. Microwave on HIGH (100%) about 2 minutes, pausing to stir, or until mixture thickens. Pour over pumpkin; microwave, uncovered, on HIGH (100%) 1 minute.

GREEK-STYLE SNOW PEAS

This recipe was tested in a 600-watt microwave oven.

200g snow peas, trimmed
30g butter
1 medium (150g) onion, thinly sliced
1 clove garlic, crushed
3 small (400g) tomatoes, chopped
1 teaspoon chopped fresh thyme
½ cup (80g) seeded black olives
150g fetta cheese, cubed

Rinse snow peas under cold water, place in shallow microwave-safe dish; cover. Microwave on HIGH (100%) 2 minutes, pausing to stir; drain, reserve.

Combine butter, onion and garlic in same dish. Microwave, covered, on HIGH (100%) about 3 minutes, pausing to stir, or until onion is soft. Stir in tomatoes and thyme; microwave, covered, on HIGH (100%) 2 minutes or until hot. Stir in snow peas, olives and cheese.

PARSNIP AND SAGE PUREE

This recipe was tested in a 600-watt microwave oven.

8 medium (1kg) parsnips, chopped
1 tablespoon water
15g butter
1 medium (150g) onion, chopped
1 clove garlic, crushed
½ cup (125ml) cream
2 tablespoons olive oil
1 tablespoon chopped fresh sage

Combine parsnips with water in large microwave-safe dish; cover. Microwave on HIGH (100%) about 8 minutes, pausing to stir, or until tender.

Place butter in medium microwave-safe dish; microwave, uncovered, on HIGH (100%) about 30 seconds or until butter is melted. Add onion and garlic; microwave, uncovered, on HIGH (100%) about 3 minutes, pausing to stir, or until onion is soft. Blend or process parsnips, onion mixture, cream and oil until smooth; stir in sage.

BROCCOLI WITH PINE NUTS

This recipe was tested in a 600-watt microwave oven.

400g broccoli
1 teaspoon vegetable oil
2 tablespoons pine nuts
3 bacon rashers, finely chopped
¼ cup (30g) grated cheddar cheese
¼ cup (20g) grated
 parmesan cheese

Cut broccoli into florets; rinse under cold water. Arrange florets in shallow microwave-safe dish, stem ends facing outer edge; cover. Microwave on HIGH (100%) about 3 minutes or until just tender.

Combine oil and nuts on microwave-safe plate; microwave, uncovered, on HIGH (100%) about 5 minutes, pausing to stir, or until nuts are browned. Place bacon on 3 sheets of absorbent paper on microwave-safe plate. Top bacon with 1 sheet paper; microwave on HIGH (100%) 3 minutes or until bacon is crisp.

Sprinkle cheeses, bacon and pine nuts over broccoli; microwave, uncovered, on HIGH (100%) about 1 minute or until cheeses are melted.

ASPARAGUS WITH HOLLANDAISE SAUCE

This recipe was tested in an 830-watt microwave oven.

500g asparagus
1 tablespoon water
125g butter, chopped
2 egg yolks
1½ tablespoons water, extra
1 tablespoon lemon juice
pinch cayenne pepper

Snap tough ends from asparagus. Arrange asparagus, in no more than 2 layers, in large microwave-safe dish, stem ends facing outer edge, sprinkle with water; cover. Microwave on HIGH (100%) 4 minutes; drain.

Place butter in microwave-safe jug; cover. Microwave on HIGH (100%) about 45 seconds or until butter is melted. Whisk egg yolks, extra water and juice in small microwave-safe bowl; microwave, uncovered, on MEDIUM (50%) 1 minute, whisking every 15 seconds, or until mixture is thickened (if mixture curdles, whisk vigorously to reconstitute). Remove from microwave; start adding melted butter, a few drops at a time, whisking constantly, until mixture starts to thicken. Continue to add butter, in a thin stream, whisking constantly, until all butter is used; whisk in pepper. Serve over asparagus.

Small bowls and spoon from House In Newtown

CLOCKWISE FROM TOP RIGHT:
Greek-Style Snow Peas;
Parsnip and Sage Puree;
Asparagus with Hollandaise Sauce; Ginger Cream Pumpkin;
Broccoli with Pine Nuts.

The recipes here are best made just before serving. None can be frozen, and each serves 4 to 6.

Sweet Things

Like many of the best things in life, desserts may not be necessities but they're certainly essential indulgences! Plus they delectably prove you care enough about your friends and family to make a fabulous final course: a sublime lemon tart, a classic creme brulee, a sinfully decadent chocolate fudge – sweet dreams are made of these.

CREME CARAMEL

3/4 cup (165g) caster sugar
3/4 cup (180ml) water
6 eggs
2 teaspoons vanilla essence
1/3 cup (75g) caster sugar, extra
1 3/4 cups (430ml) milk
300ml cream

Combine sugar and water in medium pan; stir over heat, without boiling, until sugar is dissolved. Boil, uncovered, without stirring, about 5 minutes or until syrup is golden brown. Pour syrup into deep 20cm round cake pan.

Whisk eggs, essence and extra sugar in medium bowl. Combine milk and cream in pan, stir over low heat until mixture almost boils. Gradually whisk hot milk mixture into egg mixture, strain into jug; pour mixture over caramel in pan. Place pan in baking dish with enough boiling water to come halfway up sides of pan.

Bake in moderately slow oven for about 40 minutes or until custard is just set. Remove pan from water; cool to room temperature. Cover; refrigerate overnight. Just before serving, turn Creme Caramel onto serving dish.

Serves 6 to 8.

■ Best made a day ahead.
■ Storage: Covered, in refrigerator.
■ Freeze: Not suitable.
■ Microwave: Not suitable.

CREME BRULEE

1 vanilla bean
600ml cream
6 egg yolks
1/4 cup (55g) caster sugar
1 tablespoon caster sugar, extra

Halve vanilla bean lengthways; heat split bean and cream in medium heatproof bowl over pan of simmering water.

Beat egg yolks and sugar in small bowl with electric mixer until light and creamy; gradually whisk in warm cream. Place mixture in medium pan; stir over heat, without boiling, about 5 minutes or until mixture thickens slightly and coats the spoon. Discard vanilla bean; divide mixture among six 1/3-cup (80ml) heatproof dishes. Cover; refrigerate several hours or overnight.

Place dishes in shallow baking dish filled with ice-cubes. Sprinkle custards evenly with extra sugar; place under hot grill about 2 minutes or until sugar is golden brown.

Serves 6.

■ Best prepared a day ahead.
■ Storage: Covered, in refrigerator.
■ Freeze: Not suitable.
■ Microwave: Not suitable.

OPPOSITE FROM TOP: Creme Caramel; Creme Brulee.

China from Royal Doulton; canisters and spoon from Home & Garden on the Mall; napkins from Corso De' Fiori

LEMON TART

You need about 3 lemons for this tart, and you'll find it tastes even better if made the day before required.

1¼ cups (185g) plain flour
⅓ cup (55g) icing sugar mixture
¼ cup (30g) ground almonds
125g cold butter, chopped
1 egg yolk

LEMON FILLING
1 tablespoon finely grated
lemon rind
½ cup (125ml) lemon juice
5 eggs
¾ cup (165g) caster sugar
1 cup (250ml) thickened cream

Blend or process flour, sugar, almonds and butter until combined; add egg yolk, process until ingredients just come together. Knead dough on floured surface until smooth; wrap in plastic, refrigerate for 30 minutes.

Roll pastry between sheets of baking paper until large enough to line 24cm round loose-based flan tin. Lift pastry into tin; press into side, trim edge. Cover; refrigerate 1 hour.

Cover pastry with baking paper, fill with dried beans or rice, place on oven tray. Bake in moderately hot oven 15 minutes. Remove paper and beans, bake for about 10 minutes or until browned lightly; cool. Pour Lemon Filling into pastry case then bake in moderate oven about 30 minutes or until filling has set slightly; cool. Refrigerate until cold; dust with sifted icing sugar, if desired.

Lemon Filling: Whisk all ingredients in medium bowl; stand 5 minutes.

Serves 8.

- Best made a day ahead.
- Storage: Covered, in refrigerator.
- Freeze: Not suitable.
- Microwave: Not suitable.

BELOW: Lemon Tart.
OPPOSITE: Tiramisu.

TIRAMISU

2 tablespoons instant coffee powder
1¼ cups (310ml) boiling water
1 cup (250ml) Marsala
250g packet sponge-finger biscuits
½ cup (125ml) thickened cream
⅓ cup (55g) icing sugar mixture
2 cups (500g) mascarpone cheese
40g dark chocolate, grated

Dissolve coffee powder in the boiling water in medium bowl; stir in ⅔ cup (160ml) of the Marsala. Cool. Dip half of the biscuits, 1 at a time, in coffee mixture then arrange them, in a single layer, in a 2.5-litre (10-cup) glass dish.

Beat cream and icing sugar in small bowl until soft peaks form; fold in the mascarpone and remaining Marsala.

Spread half the cream mixture over biscuits in dish. Dip remaining biscuits in remaining coffee mixture; arrange on top cream layer. Top biscuit layer with remaining cream mixture; sprinkle with chocolate. Cover; refrigerate for several hours or overnight. Decorate with strawberries, if desired.

Serves 6.

■ Best made a day ahead.
■ Storage: Covered, in refrigerator.
■ Freeze: Not suitable.
■ Microwave: Not suitable.

45

CHOCOLATE HEDGEHOG SLICE

150g butter
2/3 cup (150g) caster sugar
1/4 cup (25g) cocoa powder
1/3 cup (30g) desiccated coconut
1 egg, lightly beaten
250g packet Milk Coffee Biscuits, coarsely chopped
1/2 cup (60g) chopped pecans

Grease 19cm x 29cm rectangular slice pan, line base with baking paper, extending 2cm over edge of long sides of pan.

Combine butter, sugar and sifted cocoa in medium pan; stir over heat until butter is melted. Remove from heat; stir in coconut, egg, biscuits and nuts, press mixture into prepared pan. Cover; refrigerate several hours or overnight. Turn onto board before cutting.

- Best made a day ahead.
- Storage: Airtight container.
- Freeze: Suitable.
- Microwave: Suitable.

BISCUIT CREAM LOG

2 cups (500ml) thickened cream
1/4 cup (40g) icing sugar mixture
1 1/2 tablespoons Kahlua or Tia Maria
200g packet Choc Crunch biscuits

Beat cream, sifted icing sugar and liqueur in small bowl with electric mixer until firm peaks form.

Sandwich biscuits together with cream mixture, shaping into log on serving plate. Cover log with remaining cream mixture, using a spatula to give a rough texture. Cover loosely; refrigerate overnight. Decorate with sifted drinking chocolate and halved strawberries, if desired; slice on the diagonal.

Serves 6 to 8.

- Best made a day ahead.
- Storage: Covered, in refrigerator.
- Freeze: Not suitable.
- Microwave: Not suitable.

BISCOTTEN TORTE

24 Milk Coffee biscuits
1/2 cup (125ml) milk
1 1/2 tablespoons rum
300ml thickened cream

GROUND ALMOND FILLING
2 eggs, separated
125g butter, chopped
1/2 cup (110g) caster sugar
few drops almond essence
1 cup (125g) ground almonds
1/2 cup (125ml) milk

Arrange 6 biscuits lengthways, in 2 rows of 3 each, on a sheet of foil; brush the biscuits generously with combined milk and rum. Spread biscuits with a third of Ground Almond Filling. Repeat layering with the remaining biscuits, milk mixture and filling, ending with a final layer of biscuits. Wrap torte in foil; refrigerate 8 hours or overnight.

Beat cream in small bowl with electric mixer until soft peaks form. Cover torte with cream, running a fork lightly through cream to give swirled effect. Decorate with dark and white chocolate curls, if desired.

Ground Almond Filling: Beat egg whites in small bowl with electric mixer until soft peaks form; reserve. Combine butter, sugar, essence and egg yolks in medium bowl with electric mixer; do not overmix. Stir in almonds; gradually beat in milk with electric mixer. Gently fold egg whites into almond mixture.

Serves 6 to 8.

- Best made a day ahead.
- Storage: Covered, in refrigerator.
- Freeze: Not suitable.
- Microwave: Not suitable.

CLOCKWISE FROM TOP: Biscotten Torte;
Chocolate Hedgehog Slice;
Biscuit Cream Log.

China from Villeroy & Boch

CITRUS MERINGUE TRIFLE

Cointreau or Grand Marnier can be added to this recipe by substituting 1/3 cup (80ml) of one or the other for 1/3 cup (80ml) of the orange juice used with the lemon butter mixture.

1 cup (250ml) orange juice
3/4 cup (180ml) lemon butter
**2 x 250g packets sponge-
   finger biscuits**

CITRUS FILLING
1/2 cup (125ml) orange juice
1/4 cup (60ml) lemon juice
3 x 250g packets light cream cheese
1/2 cup (80g) icing sugar mixture
300ml thickened cream

MERINGUE
4 egg whites
3/4 cup (165g) caster sugar

Combine juice and lemon butter in pan; stir over low heat until smooth. Cool to room temperature.

Dip half the biscuits in lemon-butter mixture then place them, in a single layer, in a 2.5-litre (10-cup) heatproof dish. Spread half the Citrus Filling over biscuits. Dip remaining biscuits in lemon-butter mixture; layer over filling. Brush biscuits with any remaining lemon-butter mixture; top biscuits with the remaining filling. Cover, refrigerate overnight.

Spread meringue over trifle; put under grill or bake in moderate oven about 5 minutes or until browned. Refrigerate.
Citrus Filling: Beat juices, cream cheese and sugar in large bowl with electric mixer until smooth. Beat cream in small bowl with electric mixer until soft peaks form; fold cream into cream-cheese mixture.

Meringue: Beat egg whites in small bowl with electric mixer until soft peaks form. Gradually add sugar, beating until dissolved between additions.

Serves 6 to 8.

- Citrus Meringue Trifle, without Meringue, best made a day ahead. Top with Meringue up to 4 hours before serving.
- Storage, Covered, in refrigerator.
- Freeze: Not suitable.
- Microwave: Not suitable.

ABOVE: Citrus Meringue Trifle.
OPPOSITE: Flourless Chocolate Dessert Cake.

FLOURLESS CHOCOLATE DESSERT CAKE

This crusty-topped cake will sink slightly as it cools.

100g dark chocolate
100g unsalted butter
2 tablespoons Marsala
⅔ cup (150g) caster sugar
⅔ cup (80g) ground almonds
1 tablespoon instant coffee powder
1 tablespoon hot water
3 eggs, separated
icing sugar mixture

STRAWBERRY COULIS
250g strawberries
¼ cup (40g) icing sugar mixture

Grease a deep 20cm round cake pan, line base and side with baking paper.

Combine chocolate and butter in small pan; stir over low heat until both are melted. Combine chocolate mixture with Marsala, caster sugar, almonds and combined coffee and water in large bowl; beat in egg yolks, 1 at a time. Beat egg whites in small bowl with electric mixer until soft peaks form; gently fold into chocolate mixture, in 2 batches. Pour mixture into prepared pan.

Bake in moderate oven 50 minutes; cover with foil during baking if over-browning. Cool cake in pan, cover; refrigerate several hours or overnight. Carefully turn cake onto board; cut into slices with a hot knife. Dust cake with sifted icing sugar mixture; serve with Strawberry Coulis.

Strawberry Coulis: Blend or process hulled strawberries and icing sugar until mixture is smooth.

Serves 6.

■ Both Flourless Chocolate Dessert Cake and Strawberry Coulis best made a day ahead.
■ Storage: Covered, separately, in refrigerator.
■ Freeze: Cake suitable.
■ Microwave: Not suitable.

MICROWAVE MOCHA SELF-SAUCING PUDDING

This recipe was tested in an 830-watt microwave oven.

60g butter
1½ cups (225g) self-raising flour
1 cup (220g) caster sugar
½ cup (50g) cocoa powder
¾ cup (180ml) milk
1 cup (200g) firmly packed brown sugar
2 teaspoons instant coffee powder
2 cups (500ml) boiling water

Place butter in a 3-litre (12-cup) microwave-safe dish; microwave on HIGH (100%) about 1 minute or until butter is melted. Stir in combined sifted flour, caster sugar and half the cocoa with all the milk; beat until smooth. Sift the remaining cocoa, brown sugar and the coffee powder evenly over the top; carefully pour boiling water over sugar mixture. Microwave, uncovered, on HIGH (100%) about 12 minutes or until just cooked in centre; stand 5 minutes before serving.

Serves 4 to 6.

■ Best made just before serving.
■ Freeze: Not suitable.

MICROWAVE GOLDEN-SYRUP SELF-SAUCING PUDDING

This recipe was tested in an 830-watt microwave oven.

60g butter
1½ cups (225g) self-raising flour
¾ cup (165g) caster sugar
2 tablespoons golden syrup
¾ cup (180ml) milk
1 cup (200g) firmly packed brown sugar
2 cups (500ml) boiling water

Place butter in a 3-litre (12-cup) microwave-safe dish; microwave on HIGH (100%) about 1 minute or until butter is melted. Stir in sifted flour, caster sugar, golden syrup and milk; beat until smooth. Sift brown sugar evenly on top, carefully pour boiling water over brown sugar. Microwave, uncovered, on HIGH (100%) about 12 minutes or until just cooked in centre; stand 5 minutes before serving.

Serves 4 to 6.

■ Best made just before serving.
■ Freeze: Not suitable.

MICROWAVE LEMON AND BLUEBERRY SELF-SAUCING PUDDING

This recipe was tested in an 830-watt microwave oven.

60g butter
1½ cups (225g) self-raising flour
1 cup (220g) caster sugar
1 tablespoon grated lemon rind
¾ cup (180ml) milk
1 cup (150g) fresh blueberries
1 cup (200g) firmly packed brown sugar
½ cup (125ml) lemon juice
1½ cups (375ml) boiling water

Place butter in a 3-litre (12-cup) microwave-safe dish; microwave on HIGH (100%) about 1 minute or until butter is melted. Stir in sifted flour, caster sugar, rind and milk, beat until smooth; stir in blueberries. Sift brown sugar evenly over top; carefully pour combined juice and boiling water over brown sugar. Microwave, uncovered, on HIGH (100%) about 12 minutes or until just cooked in centre; stand 5 minutes before serving.

Serves 4 to 6.

■ Best made just before serving.
■ Freeze: Not suitable.

China from Accoutrement; tray at back from Corso De' Fiori

CLOCKWISE FROM TOP: Microwave Golden-Syrup Self-Saucing Pudding; Microwave Lemon and Blueberry Self-Saucing Pudding; Microwave Mocha Self-Saucing Pudding.

Platter, cloth and napkins from Mosmania

RICH CHOCOLATE SELF-SAUCING PUDDING

1 cup (150g) self-raising flour
3/4 cup (165g) caster sugar
2 tablespoons cocoa powder
1/2 cup (125ml) milk
1 teaspoon vanilla essence
30g butter, melted
3/4 cup (150g) firmly packed
   brown sugar
1/4 cup (25g) cocoa powder, extra
1 3/4 cups (430ml) hot water

Grease 2-litre (8-cup) ovenproof dish.

Sift flour, caster sugar and cocoa into large bowl; add the combined milk, essence and butter, stir until smooth. Pour mixture into prepared dish; sift combined brown sugar and extra cocoa evenly over top. Carefully pour hot water over pudding.

Bake in a moderate oven for about 50 minutes or until pudding is firm. Dust with sifted icing sugar, if desired.

Serves 4 to 6.

▪ Best made just before serving.
▪ Freeze: Not suitable
▪ Microwave : Not suitable.

MARS BAR CHEESECAKE

250g packet plain chocolate biscuits
150g butter, melted
3 teaspoons gelatine
1/4 cup (60ml) water
375g packaged cream
   cheese, softened
1 teaspoon vanilla essence
1/2 cup (110g) caster sugar
300ml thickened cream
3 x 60g Mars Bars, finely chopped

Line base of 24cm springform tin with foil.

Process biscuits until finely crushed; add butter, process until just combined. Press biscuit mixture evenly over base and side of the prepared tin. Cover; refrigerate 1 hour.

Sprinkle gelatine over water in cup, stand in pan of simmering water, stir until dissolved; cool.

Beat cheese, essence and sugar in small bowl with electric mixer until smooth. Beat cream in separate small bowl until soft peaks form. Stir gelatine mixture into cheese mixture with Mars Bars; fold in cream. Pour mixture into tin; refrigerate until set.

Serves 8 to 10.

▪ Can be made 2 days ahead.
▪ Storage: Covered, in refrigerator.
▪ Freeze: Not suitable.
▪ Microwave: Gelatine suitable.

ABOVE: Rich Chocolate Self-Saucing Pudding.
OPPOSITE: Mars Bar Cheesecake.

BAKED LEMON CHEESECAKE

250g packet plain sweet biscuits
125g butter, melted
3 eggs
½ cup (110g) caster sugar
3 x 250g packets cream
 cheese, softened
1 tablespoon grated lemon rind
¼ cup (60ml) lemon juice

Line base of 22cm springform tin with foil.

Process biscuits until finely crushed; add butter, process until just combined. Press biscuit mixture evenly over base and side of prepared tin, leaving 5mm border, cover; refrigerate 1 hour.

Beat eggs and sugar in medium bowl with electric mixer until thick and creamy; add cheese, rind and juice, beat until smooth. Place springform tin on oven tray; pour cheese mixture into tin.

Bake in moderate oven about 1 hour or until firm. Cool in oven with the door ajar. Cover cheesecake; refrigerate several hours or overnight.

Serves 8 to 10.

■ Can be made a day ahead.
■ Storage: Covered, in refrigerator.
■ Freeze: Not suitable.
■ Microwave: Not suitable.

BAKED BANANA CHEESECAKE

You need about 3 large (700g)
overripe bananas for this recipe.

1½ cups (225g) plain flour
¼ cup (40g) icing sugar mixture
90g butter
2 egg yolks
1 tablespoon water, approximately

BANANA FILLING
2 x 250g packets cream
 cheese, softened
½ cup (110g) caster sugar
1½ cups mashed banana
3 eggs, lightly beaten
2 teaspoons vanilla essence
1 tablespoon rum, optional

Grease 22cm springform tin.

Sift dry ingredients together; rub in butter, add egg yolks and enough water to make ingredients cling together. Press mixture into a ball; knead on floured surface until smooth. Cover with plastic; refrigerate 30 minutes.

Press pastry evenly into prepared tin to cover base and side, trim edge, lightly prick base with fork. Cover; refrigerate 30 minutes.

Cover pastry with baking paper, fill with dried beans or rice. Bake in moderately hot oven 10 minutes; remove paper and beans, bake 15 minutes or until browned lightly. Cool.

Pour filling into pastry case. Bake in moderate oven about for 1¼ hours or until set; cool. Cover cheesecake; refrigerate for 3 hours or overnight.

Banana Filling: Beat cheese and sugar in medium bowl with electric mixer until smooth; add remaining ingredients, beat until smooth.

Serves 8 to 10.

■ Best made a day ahead.
■ Storage: Covered, in refrigerator.
■ Freeze: Not suitable.
■ Microwave: Not suitable.

CARAMEL CRUNCH CHEESECAKE

125g plain chocolate biscuits
60g butter, melted
2 x 250g packets cream
 cheese, softened
2 teaspoons finely grated
 lemon rind
⅓ cup (75g) caster sugar
3 eggs
⅓ cup (80ml) cream
1 tablespoon plain flour
50g bar chocolate-coated
 honeycomb, finely chopped

CARAMEL FILLING
30g butter
¼ cup (50g) firmly packed
 brown sugar
2 tablespoons sweetened
 condensed milk
1 tablespoon golden syrup
2 tablespoons hot water

CHOCOLATE TOPPING
150g dark chocolate, chopped
¼ cup (60ml) cream

Line base of 22cm springform tin with foil, line side with baking paper.

Process biscuits until finely crushed; add butter, process until just combined. Press biscuit mixture evenly over base of prepared tin, cover; refrigerate 1 hour.

Beat cream cheese, rind and sugar in medium bowl with electric mixer until smooth; add eggs, 1 at a time, beating well between additions. Add cream and flour; beat until smooth. Stir honeycomb and the Caramel Filling into cheese mixture. Place springform tin on oven tray; pour cheesecake mixture into tin.

Bake in slow oven about 1¼ hours or until firm; cool in oven with door ajar. Spread the Chocolate Topping over the cheesecake; refrigerate for 1 hour or until set.

Caramel Filling: Combine all the ingredients in small pan; stir over low heat until the sugar is dissolved. Boil, stirring occasionally, about 4 minutes or until a deep caramel colour. Cool.

Chocolate Topping: Combine the chocolate and cream in small heatproof bowl; stir over pan of simmering water until mixture is smooth. Cool.

Serves 8 to 10.

■ Can be made a day ahead.
■ Storage: Covered, in refrigerator.
■ Freeze: Not suitable.
■ Microwave: Chocolate Topping suitable.

CLOCKWISE FROM TOP: Baked Lemon Cheesecake; Baked Banana Cheesecake; Caramel Crunch Cheesecake.

Mat, cups and saucers from Freedom Furniture; napkins from Orson & Blake Collectables

CREAMY NUT FUDGE

2 x 100g packets
   white marshmallows
60g unsalted butter
1 tablespoon water
125g milk chocolate, chopped
1 teaspoon vanilla essence
1 cup (140g) slivered almonds

Grease 8cm x 26cm bar pan, line base and sides with baking paper.

Combine marshmallows, butter and water in medium pan; stir over low heat until marshmallows melt. Remove from heat, stir in chocolate and essence; when chocolate is melted, mix in nuts. Quickly pour the mixture into prepared pan; cool. Cover; refrigerate until firm.
White Chocolate Fudge: Substitute white chocolate Melts for milk chocolate.

■ Can be made 1 week ahead.
■ Storage: Covered, in refrigerator.
■ Freeze: Not suitable.
■ Microwave: Not suitable.

RICH CHOCOLATE FUDGE

You need a candy thermometer for this recipe. For best results, prepare all ingredients before beginning.

1 cup (220g) caster sugar
2/3 cup (160ml) sour cream
2 tablespoons glucose syrup
250g dark cooking chocolate,
   finely chopped
100g packet white
   marshmallows, chopped

Grease 8cm x 26cm bar pan, line base and sides with baking paper.

Combine sugar, cream and glucose in a small pan; stir over low heat until sugar is dissolved. Bring the mixture to boil then immediately simmer, stirring occasionally, until mixture reaches 105°C on candy thermometer.

Remove from heat; immediately stir in chocolate and marshmallows until both melt. Quickly pour mixture into prepared pan; cool. Cover; refrigerate until firm.

■ Can be made 3 days ahead.
■ Storage: Covered, in refrigerator.
■ Freeze: Not suitable.
■ Microwave: Not suitable.

MERINGUE ROLL

You need about 2 passionfruit for this recipe.

4 egg whites
1/2 cup (110g) caster sugar
2 tablespoons caster sugar, extra
2 cups (500ml) thickened cream
250g strawberries, halved
1 medium (85g) kiwi fruit, sliced
2 tablespoons passionfruit pulp

Grease 26cm x 32cm Swiss roll pan, line base with baking paper, extending 5cm over edge of long sides of pan.

Beat egg whites in small bowl with electric mixer until soft peaks form; add sugar, in batches, beating until dissolved between additions. Spread the mixture into prepared pan.

Bake meringue in moderately hot oven about 10 minutes or until lightly browned. Turn meringue onto sheet of baking paper sprinkled with extra sugar. Gently peel away and discard lining paper; stand meringue 2 minutes.

Beat cream in small bowl with electric mixer until soft peaks form. Spread a third of the cream over the slightly warm meringue. Place half the strawberry halves lengthways along centre of meringue; roll meringue firmly from long side, using paper as a guide. Cover; refrigerate 30 minutes. Trim ends, cover meringue roll with remaining cream; decorate with remaining strawberries, kiwi fruit and passionfruit pulp. Cover; refrigerate until ready to serve.

Serves 6.

■ Can be made 3 hours ahead.
■ Storage: Covered, in refrigerator.
■ Freeze: Not suitable.
■ Microwave: Not suitable.

OPPOSITE FROM TOP: Rich Chocolate Fudge; Creamy Nut Fudge with White Chocolate Fudge variation.
RIGHT: Meringue Roll.

BANANA CARAMEL TART

1 cup (150g) plain flour
60g cold butter, chopped
2 tablespoons caster sugar
1 egg yolk
1 tablespoon cold water,
    approximately
2 medium (400g) bananas,
    thinly sliced
300ml thickened cream
1 tablespoon desiccated
    coconut, toasted

CARAMEL FILLING
1 cup (200g) firmly packed
    brown sugar
125g butter, chopped
1 tablespoon boiling water
1/4 cup (35g) cornflour
1 cup (250ml) milk
2 egg yolks
1 teaspoon vanilla essence

Grease 24cm loose-based flan tin.

Sift flour into medium bowl, rub in butter. Add sugar, egg yolk and enough water to mix to a soft dough. Knead dough on floured surface until smooth, wrap in plastic; refrigerate 30 minutes.

Roll pastry between sheets of baking paper until large enough to line prepared tin. Lift pastry into tin; press into side, trim edge, lightly prick base with fork. Cover pastry with baking paper, fill with dried beans or rice. Bake in moderately hot oven 10 minutes; remove paper and beans, bake for 10 minutes or until browned lightly. Cool.

Spread Caramel Filling into pastry case, top with banana slices then whipped cream; sprinkle with coconut. Refrigerate 1 hour before serving.

Caramel Filling: Combine sugar, butter and water in medium pan; stir over low heat until sugar is dissolved and butter

melted. Add the blended cornflour and milk; stir over heat until mixture boils and thickens. Remove from heat; quickly whisk in egg yolks and essence. Cover; cool.

Serves 6 to 8.

▧ Can be made a day ahead.
▧ Storage: Covered, in refrigerator.
▧ Freeze: Not suitable.
▧ Microwave: Not suitable.

ABOVE: Banana Caramel Tart.
OPPOSITE: Sticky Date Pudding with Butterscotch Sauce.

STICKY DATE PUDDING WITH BUTTERSCOTCH SAUCE

1¼ cups (210g) seeded dates
1¼ cups (310ml) boiling water
1 teaspoon bicarbonate of soda
60g butter, chopped
¾ cup (150g) firmly packed
    brown sugar
2 eggs
1 cup (150g) self-raising flour

BUTTERSCOTCH SAUCE
1 cup (200g) firmly packed
    brown sugar
300ml cream
200g butter

Grease deep 20cm round cake pan, line base with baking paper.

Combine dates and water in pan; bring to boil then immediately remove from heat. Stir in the soda; allow to stand 5 minutes. Blend or process the date mixture with butter and sugar until almost smooth; add eggs and flour, blend or process until just combined. Pour mixture into prepared pan.

Bake in moderate oven about 55 minutes or until cooked through; cover with foil during baking if over-browning. Stand pudding 10 minutes before turning out of pan; serve with Butterscotch Sauce poured over top.

Butterscotch Sauce: Combine ingredients in medium pan; stir over low heat until sugar is dissolved and butter melted.

Serves 6 to 8.

- Sticky Date Pudding and Butterscotch Sauce can be made a day ahead.
- Storage: Pudding, in airtight container. Sauce, covered, in refrigerator.
- Freeze: Pudding suitable.
- Microwave: Sauce suitable.

Baking

Nothing is more comfortingly homey and appetite-provoking than the smell of baking emanating from your oven – the sugary, bittersweet scent of a chocolate cake or the full, yeasty aroma of a loaf of toasty homemade bread wafting through your house will lead everyone by the nose straight into the kitchen.

MISSISSIPPI MUD CAKE

250g cold unsalted butter, chopped
150g dark chocolate, chopped
2 cups (440g) caster sugar
1 cup (250ml) hot water
⅓ cup (80ml) whisky
1 tablespoon instant coffee powder
1½ cups (225g) plain flour
¼ cup (35g) self-raising flour
¼ cup (25g) cocoa powder
2 eggs, lightly beaten

Grease 23cm square slab pan, line base with baking paper.

Combine butter, chocolate, sugar, water, whisky and coffee powder in medium pan; stir over low heat until chocolate is melted. Transfer mixture to large bowl; cool. Stir in sifted flours and cocoa, then eggs; pour mixture into prepared pan.

Bake in moderately slow oven for 1¼ hours. Stand cake 30 minutes; turn onto wire rack to cool. Serve dusted with sifted icing sugar.

▓ Can be made 3 days ahead.
▓ Storage: Covered, in refrigerator.
▓ Freeze: Suitable.
▓ Microwave: Chocolate mixture suitable.

LEMON SOUR CREAM CAKE

For best results, use butter, eggs and sour cream at room temperature.

125g butter
2 teaspoons finely grated lemon rind
1 cup (220g) caster sugar
3 eggs
1 cup (150g) plain flour
1/2 teaspoon baking powder
1/3 cup (80ml) sour cream

Grease 14cm x 21cm loaf pan, line base with baking paper.

Beat butter, rind and sugar in small bowl with electric mixer until light and fluffy. Add eggs, 1 at a time, beating until just combined between additions (the mixture might curdle at this stage). Transfer mixture to large bowl, stir in sifted flour and baking powder with sour cream; spread mixture into prepared pan. Bake in moderately slow oven 1 hour. Stand cake 5 minutes; turn onto wire rack to cool.

- Can be made 3 days ahead.
- Storage: Airtight container.
- Freeze: Suitable.
- Microwave: Not suitable.

ORANGE POPPY SEED CAKE

1/4 cup (40g) poppy seeds
1/4 cup (60ml) milk
185g butter
1 1/2 tablespoons finely grated orange rind
1 1/4 cups (275g) caster sugar
3 eggs
3/4 cup (105g) plain flour
3/4 cup (105g) self-raising flour
1/2 cup (60g) ground almonds
1/3 cup (80ml) orange juice

ORANGE CREAM
500g packaged cream cheese, softened
1/2 cup (125ml) sour cream
2 tablespoons finely grated orange rind
3/4 cup (120g) icing sugar mixture
1 tablespoon orange juice

Grease deep 22cm round cake pan, line base with baking paper.

Combine seeds and milk in small bowl, stand 20 minutes. Beat butter, rind and sugar in small bowl with electric mixer until light and fluffy. Add eggs, 1 at a time, beating until just combined between additions. Transfer mixture to large bowl, stir in sifted flours, almonds, undrained poppy seeds and juice; spread mixture in prepared pan.

Bake in moderate oven 45 minutes. Stand cake 5 minutes; turn onto wire rack to cool. Split the cake into 3 layers; sandwich layers with half the Orange Cream, cover top and side of cake with remaining Orange Cream.

Orange Cream: Beat cheese, cream and rind in medium bowl with electric mixer until smooth; beat in sifted icing sugar and juice, in 3 batches.

- Uniced cake can be made 2 days ahead.
- Storage: Airtight container.
- Freeze: Cake suitable.
- Microwave: Not suitable.

OPPOSITE FROM TOP: Orange Poppy Seed Cake; Lemon Sour Cream Cake.

Blue plate from The Bay Tree Kitchen Shop

LUMBERJACK CAKE

2 large (400g) apples, peeled, finely chopped
1 cup (160g) chopped pitted dates
1 teaspoon bicarbonate of soda
1 cup (250ml) boiling water
125g butter
1 teaspoon vanilla essence
1 cup (220g) caster sugar
1 egg
1½ cups (225g) plain flour

COCONUT TOPPING
60g butter
½ cup (100g) firmly packed brown sugar
½ cup (125ml) milk
⅔ cup (50g) shredded coconut

Grease deep 19cm square cake pan, line base with baking paper.

Combine apples, dates, soda and water in medium bowl; cover, stand 10 minutes. Beat butter, essence and sugar in small bowl with electric mixer until light and fluffy; add egg, beat until combined. Transfer mixture to a large bowl, stir in sifted flour alternately with apple mixture; spread mixture into prepared pan. Bake in moderate oven 50 minutes. Pour over warm Coconut Topping; bake about 30 minutes or until golden brown. Cool cake in pan.

Coconut Topping: Combine butter, sugar and milk in small pan; stir over low heat until butter is melted and sugar dissolved. Stir in coconut.

- Can be made 3 days ahead.
- Storage: Airtight container, in refrigerator.
- Freeze: Suitable.
- Microwave: Not suitable.

HUMMINGBIRD CAKE

You need about 2 large (460g) overripe bananas for this recipe.

450g can crushed pineapple in heavy syrup
1 cup (150g) plain flour
½ cup (75g) self-raising flour
½ teaspoon bicarbonate of soda
½ teaspoon ground cinnamon
½ teaspoon ground ginger
1 cup (200g) firmly packed brown sugar
½ cup (45g) desiccated coconut
1 cup mashed banana
2 eggs, lightly beaten
¾ cup (180ml) vegetable oil

LEMON FROSTING
200g packaged cream cheese, softened
2 teaspoons grated lemon rind
½ cup (80g) icing sugar mixture
3 teaspoons lemon juice

Grease deep 19cm square cake pan, line base with baking paper.

Drain pineapple well, reserve ¼ cup (60ml) syrup. Sift both the flours, soda,

Cake plate from The Bay Tree Kitchen Shop; tray from Freedom Furniture

Platters and cake server from Kitchen Kapers; napkins from Mosmania; basket from Shack Homewares

BEETROOT CAKE

250g butter
2 teaspoons finely grated lemon rind
1 cup (220g) caster sugar
4 eggs
1 large (200g) uncooked beetroot, peeled, finely chopped
1 cup (150g) dried currants
1 tablespoon lemon juice
½ teaspoon ground nutmeg
1 cup (150g) plain flour
1 cup (150g) self-raising flour

Grease 14cm x 21cm loaf pan, line base with baking paper.

Cream butter, rind and sugar in small bowl with electric mixer until light and fluffy; add eggs, 1 at a time, beating well between additions. Transfer the mixture to large bowl; stir in beetroot, currants, juice, nutmeg and half of the sifted flours. Stir in remaining sifted flours; spread mixture into prepared pan.

Bake in moderate oven 1½ hours; cover with foil if overbrowning. Stand cake 5 minutes; turn onto wire rack.

▧ Can be made 2 days ahead.
▧ Storage: Airtight container.
▧ Freeze: Suitable.
▧ Microwave: Not suitable.

China from Villeroy & Boch

DATE AND BRAN MUFFINS

Muffins can be made and baked on the same day but will be much nicer if the mixture is refrigerated overnight and muffins baked the following day.

1¼ cups (185g) plain flour
1 teaspoon bicarbonate of soda
1 teaspoon ground cinnamon
½ cup (110g) caster sugar
1¾ cups (105g) unprocessed bran
¾ cup (120g) finely chopped dates
½ cup (125ml) vegetable oil
1½ cups (375ml) buttermilk
1 egg, lightly beaten

Sift flour, soda, cinnamon and sugar into large bowl; mix in bran and dates. Stir in remaining ingredients, taking care not to overmix (the mixture should be coarse and slightly lumpy). Cover; refrigerate overnight.

Grease a 12-hole (⅓ cup/80ml capacity) muffin pan; divide mixture among pan holes. Bake muffins in moderately hot oven for 20 minutes. Serve warm.

Makes 12.

▧ Best prepared a day ahead.
▧ Storage: Covered, in refrigerator.
▧ Freeze: Cooked muffins suitable.
▧ Microwave: Not suitable.

BLUEBERRY MUFFINS

Frozen blueberries can be used without being thawed first.

2 cups (300g) self-raising flour
¾ cup (150g) firmly packed brown sugar
1 cup (150g) fresh or frozen blueberries
1 egg, lightly beaten
¾ cup (180ml) buttermilk
½ cup (125ml) vegetable oil

Grease a 6-hole (¾ cup/180ml capacity) Texas-style muffin pan.

Sift dry ingredients into large bowl; stir in remaining ingredients, divide mixture among pan holes.

Bake muffins in moderately hot oven for 20 minutes. Dust with sifted icing sugar, if desired; serve warm.

Makes 6.

▧ Best made on day of serving.
▧ Storage: Airtight container.
▧ Freeze: Suitable.
▧ Microwave: Not suitable.

OPPOSITE: Beetroot Cake.
RIGHT FROM TOP: Date and Bran Muffins; Blueberry Muffins.

Basket, napkins, cups and saucers from Kitchen Kapers; artificial leaves from Sirocco Homewares

cinnamon and ginger into large bowl, stir in sugar and coconut. Add the pineapple, reserved syrup, banana, eggs and oil, stir until combined; spread mixture into prepared pan.

Bake in moderate oven 1 hour; cover with foil if overbrowning. Stand cake 10 minutes; turn onto wire rack. When cold, top cake with Lemon Frosting.

Lemon Frosting: Beat cream cheese and rind in small bowl with electric mixer until light and fluffy. Gradually beat in the sifted icing sugar and juice, beat until smooth.

■ Can be made a day ahead.
■ Storage: Airtight container, in refrigerator.
■ Freeze: Suitable.
■ Microwave: Not suitable.

APPLE CUSTARD TEA CAKE

200g butter, chopped
1/2 cup (110g) caster sugar
2 eggs
1 1/4 cups (185g) self-raising flour
1/3 cup (40g) custard powder
2 medium (300g) green apples, peeled, thinly sliced
1 tablespoon butter, melted, extra
2 teaspoons caster sugar, extra
1/2 teaspoon ground cinnamon

CUSTARD
2 tablespoons custard powder
1/4 cup (55g) caster sugar
1 cup (250ml) milk
20g butter
1 tablespoon vanilla essence

Grease deep 22cm round cake pan, line base with baking paper.

Beat butter and sugar in small bowl with electric mixer until light and fluffy. Add eggs, 1 at a time, beating well between additions. Stir in sifted flour and custard powder.

Spread half the mixture into prepared pan, top with Custard. Top Custard with spoonfuls of remaining cake mixture; gently spread with spatula to completely cover Custard. Arrange apples on top, brush with the extra tablespoon melted butter then sprinkle with combined extra sugar and cinnamon. Bake in moderate oven 1 1/4 hours; cool in pan.

Custard: Combine custard powder and sugar in small pan; gradually add milk, stirring over heat until mixture thickens slightly. Remove from heat, stir in butter and essence. Press plastic wrap over surface of Custard; cool. Whisk until smooth just before using.

■ Best made on day of serving.
■ Storage: Covered, in refrigerator.
■ Freeze: Suitable.
■ Microwave: Custard suitable.

OPPOSITE FROM TOP: Hummingbird Cake; Lumberjack Cake.
ABOVE: Apple Custard Tea Cake.

ABOVE: Muesli Bars.
OPPOSITE: Chocolate Mud Cake.

MUESLI BARS

90g butter
1/2 cup (125ml) golden syrup
1/2 cup (100g) firmly packed
   brown sugar
1 cup (90g) rolled oats
1/3 cup (40g) chopped hazelnuts
1/4 cup (40g) sunflower seed kernels
1/2 cup (75g) chopped dried apricots
1/3 cup (30g) desiccated coconut
1/2 teaspoon mixed spice
1 1/2 cups (85g) bran flakes
3 egg whites, lightly beaten

Line 20cm x 30cm lamington pan with baking paper, extending paper 2cm over edge of long sides of pan.

Combine butter, syrup and sugar in small pan; stir over low heat until sugar dissolves. Combine remaining ingredients in medium bowl; stir in butter mixture. Spread mixture into prepared pan.

Bake in moderate oven for about 35 minutes or until top is crisp. Cool in pan then turn slice onto oven tray, underside up; bake in moderate oven about 25 minutes or until top is crisp. Cool before cutting.

■ Can be made 3 days ahead.
■ Storage: Airtight container.
■ Freeze: Not suitable.
■ Microwave: Not suitable.

CHOCOLATE MUD CAKE

300g dark chocolate, chopped
250g butter, chopped
1 tablespoon instant coffee powder
3/4 cup (180ml) water
3/4 cup (150g) firmly packed
    brown sugar
3/4 cup (105g) plain flour
1/4 cup (35g) self-raising flour
1/4 cup (25g) cocoa powder
2 eggs, lightly beaten
1/4 cup (60ml) Kahlua or Tia Maria

Grease deep 22cm round cake pan, line base and side with baking paper.

Combine chocolate, butter, coffee powder, water and sugar in medium pan; stir over low heat until chocolate is melted. Sift flours and cocoa powder into large bowl; whisk in the chocolate mixture, eggs and liqueur. Pour mixture into prepared pan.

Bake in moderately slow oven for 1¼ hours. Cool cake in pan; cover, refrigerate overnight.

Remove cake from pan then, if desired, dust with equal parts icing sugar and cocoa, sifted together.

■ Best made a day ahead.
■ Storage: Covered, in refrigerator.
■ Freeze: Suitable.
■ Microwave: Chocolate mixture suitable.

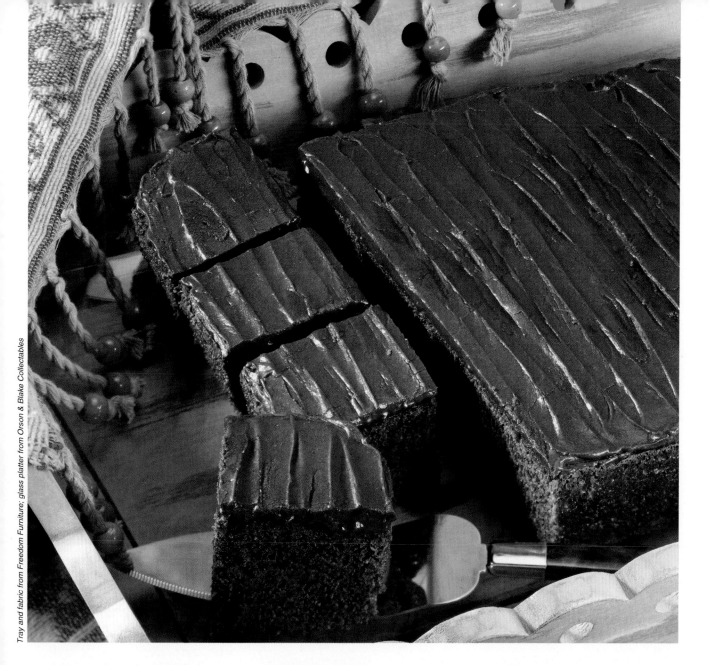

PEANUT-BUTTER COOKIES

This recipe does not contain flour. You can use crunchy or smooth peanut butter.

1 cup (260g) peanut butter
1 cup (220g) caster sugar
1 egg, lightly beaten

Combine all ingredients In medium bowl; stir until combined. Roll rounded teaspoons of mixture into balls. Place biscuits onto greased oven trays, about 5cm apart, flatten slightly with a fork.

Bake in moderate oven for about 15 minutes or until golden brown. Stand biscuits 5 minutes; turn onto wire rack to cool.

Makes about 30.

▓ Can be made a week ahead.
▓ Storage: Airtight container.
▓ Freeze: Suitable.
▓ Microwave: Not suitable.

JACKIE'S FAMILY CHOCOLATE CAKE

2 cups (500ml) water
3 cups (660g) caster sugar
250g butter, chopped
1/3 cup (35g) cocoa powder
1 teaspoon bicarbonate of soda
3 cups (450g) self-raising flour
4 eggs, lightly beaten

FUDGE FROSTING
90g butter, chopped
1/3 cup (80ml) water
1/2 cup (110g) caster sugar
1½ cups (240g) icing sugar mixture
1/3 cup (35g) cocoa powder

Grease deep 27cm x 33cm baking dish, line base with baking paper.

Combine water, sugar, butter, cocoa and soda in large pan; stir over low heat until sugar is dissolved. Boil then immediately simmer, uncovered, for 5 minutes. Transfer the mixture to large bowl; cool. Add sifted flour and eggs,

beat with electric mixer until smooth; pour mixture into prepared dish.

Bake in moderate oven 50 minutes. Stand cake 10 minutes; turn onto wire rack to cool. Spread cold cake with Fudge Frosting.

Fudge Frosting: Combine butter, water and caster sugar in small pan; stir over heat, without boiling, until the sugar is dissolved. Sift icing sugar and cocoa into medium bowl; stir in hot butter mixture, in batches. Cover; refrigerate 1 hour or until frosting has thickened. Beat until spreadable.

▓ Uniced cake can be made 3 days ahead.
▓ Storage: Airtight container.
▓ Freeze: Suitable.
▓ Microwave: Fudge Frosting suitable.

OPPOSITE: Peanut-Butter Cookies.
ABOVE: Jackie's Family Chocolate Cake.

BASIC CRISP BISCUITS

125g butter
1 teaspoon vanilla essence
3/4 cup (165g) caster sugar
1 egg yolk
1½ cups (225g) self-raising flour
2 teaspoons water

Beat butter, essence, sugar and egg yolk in small bowl with electric mixer until smooth. Stir in sifted flour and water; mix to a soft dough. Roll rounded teaspoons of mixture into balls; place about 5cm apart on greased oven trays.

Bake in moderately hot oven about 10 minutes or until browned lightly; cool on trays.

Makes about 40.

■ Can be made 4 days ahead.
■ Storage: Airtight container.
■ Freeze: Suitable.
■ Microwave: Not suitable.

ICED GINGERNUTS

1 quantity Basic Crisp Biscuit dough
2 teaspoons ground ginger
1 teaspoon ground cinnamon
1 teaspoon ground nutmeg
1/4 teaspoon ground cloves
2 tablespoons finely chopped glace ginger
1 tablespoon milk

ICING
3/4 cup (120g) icing sugar mixture
2 teaspoons treacle
2 tablespoons cream
1 teaspoon butter

Prepare the Basic Crisp Biscuit recipe, adding sifted ground ginger, cinnamon, nutmeg and cloves with the flour, and ginger and milk with the water. Mix to a soft dough. Roll rounded teaspoons of mixture into balls; place about 5cm apart on greased oven trays, flatten to 4cm rounds.

Bake in moderately hot oven about 10 minutes or until browned lightly; cool on trays. Drizzle with icing.
Icing: Combine sifted sugar with remaining ingredients in pan; stir over hot water or low heat until smooth. Do not overheat; icing mixture should just be warm.

Makes about 40.

■ Can be made 4 days ahead.
■ Storage: Airtight container.
■ Freeze: Suitable.
■ Microwave: Icing suitable.

LEMON POPPY SEED BISCUITS

You can use grated orange rind and juice and 1/2 teaspoon ground cardamom instead of lemon and ginger, if desired.

1 teaspoon water
1 teaspoon lemon juice
1 tablespoon poppy seeds
1 quantity Basic Crisp Biscuit dough
1/2 teaspoon ground ginger
1 tablespoon grated lemon rind

Combine water, juice and seeds in small bowl, stand 15 minutes. Prepare Basic Crisp Biscuit recipe, adding undrained seed mixture, ginger and rind with sifted flour and water. Roll rounded teaspoons of mixture into balls; place about 5cm apart on greased oven trays, flatten to 4cm rounds.

Bake in moderately hot oven about 10 minutes or until browned lightly; cool on trays. Dust with sifted icing sugar, if desired.

Makes about 40.

■ Can be made 4 days ahead.
■ Storage: Airtight container.
■ Freeze: Suitable.
■ Microwave: Not suitable.

BASIC CHEWY COOKIES

If you prefer more fudge-like cookies, bake only 8 minutes.

2 eggs
1 1/3 cups (265g) firmly packed brown sugar
1 teaspoon vanilla essence
1/2 cup (125ml) vegetable oil
1 cup (150g) plain flour
3/4 cup (105g) self-raising flour
1/2 teaspoon bicarbonate of soda

Beat eggs and sugar in small bowl with electric mixer about 1 minute or until mixture changes colour. Stir in essence, oil and sifted dry ingredients (the mixture will be soft). Cover bowl; refrigerate for 1 hour. Roll level tablespoons of the mixture into balls; place 6cm apart on greased oven trays.

Bake in moderately hot oven for about 10 minutes or until browned lightly. Stand for 5 minutes; turn onto wire rack to cool.

Makes about 30.

■ Can be made 4 days ahead.
■ Storage: Airtight container.
■ Freeze: Suitable.
■ Microwave: Not suitable.

CHEWY CHOC-CHUNK COOKIES

1 quantity Basic Chewy Cookie dough
1 cup (125g) chopped pecans or walnuts, toasted
3/4 cup (120g) chopped raisins
1 cup (150g) dark chocolate Melts, halved
1/2 cup (95g) white Choc Bits

Prepare Basic Chewy Cookie recipe, adding remaining ingredients with the flour. Cover bowl, refrigerate 1 hour. Roll heaped tablespoons of mixture into balls; place about 6cm apart on greased oven trays, flatten into 6cm rounds.

Bake in moderately hot oven for about 10 minutes or until browned lightly. Stand for 5 minutes; turn onto wire rack to cool.

Makes about 20.

■ Can be made 4 days ahead.
■ Storage: Airtight container.
■ Freeze: Suitable.
■ Microwave: Not suitable.

APRICOT COCONUT COOKIES

1 quantity Basic Chewy Cookie dough
2 tablespoons maple-flavoured syrup
1 cup (150g) chopped dried apricots
1 cup (90g) rolled oats
1 cup (50g) flaked coconut
1/4 cup (40g) sunflower seed kernels

Prepare Basic Chewy Cookie recipe, adding syrup with the oil and essence, and apricots, oats, coconut and kernels with the sifted dry ingredients. Cover bowl, refrigerate 1 hour. Roll level tablespoons of mixture into balls; place about 6cm apart on greased oven trays, flatten slightly.

Bake in moderately hot oven for about 10 minutes or until browned lightly. Stand for 5 minutes; turn onto wire rack to cool.

Makes about 45.

■ Can be made 4 days ahead.
■ Storage: Airtight container.
■ Freeze: Suitable.
■ Microwave: Not suitable.

CLOCKWISE FROM BELOW:
Iced Gingernuts; Basic Crisp Biscuits; Apricot Coconut Cookies; Lemon Poppy Seed Biscuits; Basic Chewy Cookies; Chewy Choc-Chunk Cookies.

NO-BOWL FIVE-CUP SLICE

1 cup (160g) sultanas
1 cup (190g) dark Choc Bits
1 cup (150g) unsalted
roasted peanuts
1 cup (90g) desiccated coconut
1 cup (250ml) sweetened
condensed milk
50g dark chocolate, melted

Line 20cm x 30cm lamington pan with baking paper, extending paper 2cm over edge of long sides of pan.

Sprinkle pan with sultanas, Choc Bits, peanuts and coconut. Drizzle with condensed milk.

Bake, covered, in a moderately hot oven for 20 minutes. Reduce heat to moderate, uncover, bake 15 minutes; cool in pan. Drizzle melted chocolate over slice; leave to set before cutting.

- Can be made a day ahead.
- Storage: Airtight container.
- Freeze: Not suitable.
- Microwave: Chocolate suitable.

EASY-MIX BREAD

2⅓ cups (350g) plain flour
1 cup (160g) wholemeal plain flour
¼ cup (40g) cracked wheat
¼ cup (15g) unprocessed bran
2 teaspoons sugar
2 teaspoons (7g) dried yeast
1 teaspoon salt
1 tablespoon vegetable oil
1⅓ cups (330ml) warm water

Grease 14cm x 21cm loaf pan.

Combine sifted flours and remaining ingredients in large bowl of electric mixer; beat with dough hook(s) on medium speed about 3 minutes or until mixture is smooth and elastic. Turn dough onto floured surface, shape into a ball. Transfer dough to oiled bowl; cover, stand in warm place about 2 hours or until doubled in size.

Knead dough on floured surface until smooth; halve dough, knead each half until smooth then place both halves in prepared pan. Cover; stand in warm place for about 1 hour or until doubled in size.

Bake in moderately hot oven about 45 minutes or until bread is browned and sounds hollow when tapped. Remove from pan; cool on wire rack.

- Best made on day of serving.
- Freeze: Suitable.
- Microwave: Not suitable.

Board, rack, knife and tin from Kitchen Kapers

OPPOSITE: No-Bowl Five-Cup Slice.
RIGHT: Easy-Mix Bread.

MOIST COCONUT CAKE

For best results, use butter, eggs, sour cream and milk at room temperature.

125g butter
1 teaspoon coconut essence
1 cup (220g) caster sugar
2 eggs
½ cup (45g) desiccated coconut
1½ cups (225g) self-raising flour
300ml sour cream
⅓ cup (80ml) milk

COCONUT ICE FROSTING
2 cups (320g) icing sugar mixture
1⅓ cups (95g) shredded coconut
2 egg whites, lightly beaten
red food colouring, optional

Grease deep 22cm round cake pan, line base with baking paper.

Beat butter, essence and sugar in small bowl with electric mixer until light and fluffy. Add eggs, 1 at a time, beating well between additions. Transfer mixture to large bowl; stir in coconut, sifted flour, and combined sour cream and milk, in 2 batches. Spread mixture into prepared pan.

Bake in moderate oven 1 hour. Stand cake 5 minutes; turn onto wire rack to cool. Spread cold cake with Coconut Ice Frosting.

Coconut Ice Frosting: Combine icing sugar with coconut and egg whites in medium bowl; mix well. If desired, tint pink with colouring.

■ Uniced cake can be made 2 days ahead.
■ Storage: Covered, in refrigerator.
■ Freeze: Uniced cake suitable.
■ Microwave: Not suitable.

TRIPLE CHOC BROWNIES

125g cold butter, chopped
200g dark chocolate, chopped
½ cup (110g) caster sugar
2 eggs, lightly beaten
1¼ cups (185g) plain flour
150g white chocolate, chopped
100g milk chocolate, chopped

Grease deep 19cm square cake pan, line base and sides with baking paper.

Combine butter and dark chocolate in medium pan; stir over low heat until melted. Cool 10 minutes. Stir in sugar and eggs, then sifted flour; mix in remaining chocolate. Spread mixture into prepared pan.

Bake in moderate oven for about 35 minutes or until mixture is firm to touch. Cool in pan. If desired, sprinkle with sifted icing sugar before cutting.

■ Can be made 3 days ahead.
■ Storage: Airtight container.
■ Freeze: Not suitable.
■ Microwave: Butter and chocolate mixture suitable.

BELOW: Moist Coconut Cake.
OPPOSITE: Triple Choc Brownies.

CARROT CAKE WITH CREAM CHEESE FROSTING

You need about 4 medium (480g) carrots for this recipe.

1 cup (250ml) vegetable oil
3/4 cup (165g) caster sugar
2 tablespoons golden syrup
2 eggs, lightly beaten
2 cups coarsely grated carrot
3/4 cup (90g) chopped walnuts
1½ cups (225g) self-raising flour
½ teaspoon bicarbonate of soda
½ teaspoon ground nutmeg
½ teaspoon ground cinnamon

CREAM CHEESE FROSTING
125g packaged cream cheese
30g soft butter
1 teaspoon grated lemon rind
1½ cups (240g) icing sugar mixture

Grease 15cm x 25cm loaf pan, line base with baking paper.

Combine oil, sugar, syrup, eggs, carrot, nuts and sifted dry ingredients in large bowl; stir well. Pour mixture into prepared pan.

Bake in moderate oven 1 hour. Stand cake 5 minutes; turn onto wire rack to cool. Spread cold cake with Cream Cheese Frosting.

Cream Cheese Frosting: Beat cream cheese, butter and rind in small bowl with electric mixer until light and fluffy; gradually beat in icing sugar.

- Uniced cake can be made 2 days ahead.
- Storage: Airtight container.
- Freeze: Suitable.
- Microwave: Not suitable.

QUICK-MIX ONION BREAD

3 cups (450g) self-raising flour
2 x 40g packets French onion soup mix
13/4 cups (430ml) buttermilk or yogurt, approximately

Grease 14cm x 21cm loaf pan.

Sift flour into large bowl; stir in soup mix and enough buttermilk to make a soft, sticky dough. Knead dough on floured surface until smooth then shape into a loaf; place in prepared pan, brush top with a little extra buttermilk.

Bake in moderate oven about 1 hour or until bread is browned and sounds hollow when tapped. Turn onto wire rack; serve warm or cold.

- Best made on day of serving.
- Storage: Airtight container.
- Freeze: Suitable.
- Microwave: Not suitable.

BEER BREAD

3¼ cups (485g) self-raising flour
2 teaspoons salt
2 teaspoons sugar
375ml bottle light beer

Grease two 14cm x 21cm loaf pans, line bases with baking paper.

Sift flour, salt and sugar into medium bowl, make a well in the centre, pour in beer all at once. Using a spoon, mix to a soft, sticky dough. Knead dough on a floured surface until smooth then divide in half; knead each half then place them in prepared pans.

Bake in moderate oven for about 50 minutes or until bread is browned and sounds hollow when tapped. Turn onto wire rack; serve warm or cold.

- Best made on day of serving.
- Storage: Airtight container.
- Freeze: Suitable.
- Microwave: Not suitable.

ABOVE: Carrot Cake with Cream Cheese Frosting.
OPPOSITE FROM TOP: Quick-Mix Onion Bread; Beer Bread.

Jams & Marmalades

Conventional and microwave methods for making jam and marmalade are given here. Read the following handy hints before beginning.

CONVENTIONAL METHOD

- Use a small aluminium, stainless steel or enamel boiler or large saucepan. Do not use a copper or unsealed cast-iron pan: the acid in the preserve will damage the metal.

- Do not leave fruit mixtures standing in an aluminium boiler or pan for more than an hour.

- Fruit mixture in boiler should be no more than 5cm deep at any stage. Fruit is simmered, covered, to soften before adding the sugar: fruit will not tenderise further after sugar is added.

- Boil jam rapidly after the sugar has dissolved. Do not stir, but use wooden spoon to check that the jam is not sticking to the base of the boiler, especially towards the end of cooking time.

MICROWAVE METHOD

- As a guide, do not microwave more than 500g soft fruit (such as berries) or 1kg firmer fruit (such as stone fruit) at a time.

- Usually only a small amount of liquid is added to jam made in the microwave, as evaporation is minimal with microwave cooking.

- Always use a large, wide-mouthed container. Do not use plastic microwave-ware because hot jam can melt or distort the plastic.

- Check and stir the preserve occasionally towards the end of cooking time to prevent burning in a particular spot.

Sauces & Preserves

Using the best of each season's fruit and vegetables to make your own pickles, salad dressings, marmalades and jams is smart economically and satisfying emotionally. Here is just a tantalising sample of the myriad delicious and inventive possibilities of preserving food for the future.

MICROWAVE TOMATO JAM

This recipe was tested in an 850-watt microwave oven.

4 medium (750g) tomatoes, peeled
**1 small (130g) apple, peeled,
   coarsely grated**
**1/3 cup (65g) finely chopped
   glace ginger**
1/4 cup (60ml) lemon juice
2 cups (440g) sugar

Roughly chop tomatoes, combine with apple and ginger in large microwave-safe bowl. Microwave, uncovered, on HIGH (100%) for about 15 minutes or until mixture is pulpy. Add juice and sugar; stir until sugar is dissolved. Microwave, uncovered, on HIGH (100%) about 25 minutes or until jam jells when tested. Stand 5 minutes. Pour into hot sterilised jars; seal while hot.

Makes about 1 litre (4 cups).

■ Storage: In a cool, dark place for about 6 months; refrigerate after opening.

TOMATO JAM

8 medium (1.5kg) tomatoes, peeled
**2 small (260g) apples, peeled,
   coarsely grated**
**2/3 cup (130g) finely chopped
   glace ginger**
1/2 cup (125ml) lemon juice
4 cups (880g) sugar

Roughly chop tomatoes, combine with apple and ginger in small boiler or large pan. Simmer, uncovered, about 20 minutes or until mixture is pulpy. Add juice and sugar; cook, stirring over heat, without boiling, until sugar is dissolved. Bring to boil; boil rapidly, uncovered, without stirring, about 35 minutes or until jam jells when tested. Stand 5 minutes. Pour into hot sterilised jars; seal while hot.

Makes about 1.5 litres (6 cups).

■ Storage: In a cool, dark place for about 6 months; refrigerate after opening.

FRUIT SALAD JAM

You will need 3 large bananas and about 3 passionfruit for this recipe.

1²/₃ cups (250g) dried apricots
2 cups (500ml) water
**1 cup (250ml) undrained
crushed pineapple**
½ cup (125ml) orange juice
¼ cup (60ml) passionfruit pulp
3 cups (660g) caster sugar
2 cups sliced bananas

Put apricots and water in medium bowl; cover, stand 3 hours or overnight. Combine undrained apricots with pineapple in small boiler or large pan; simmer, covered, 15 minutes. Add juice and passionfruit pulp; simmer, covered, 10 minutes. Add sugar; cook, stirring over heat, without boiling, until sugar is dissolved. Add bananas, bring to boil; boil, uncovered, stirring occasionally, about 20 minutes or until jam jells when tested. Stand 5 minutes. Pour into hot, sterilised jars; seal while hot.

Microwave Fruit Salad Jam: Put apricots and water in large microwave-safe bowl; microwave, uncovered, on HIGH (100%) 5 minutes then stand 10 minutes. Stir in pineapple; microwave, uncovered, on HIGH (100%) 15 minutes. Stir in juice and pulp; microwave, uncovered, on HIGH (100%) for 10 minutes. Add sugar, stir until it is dissolved. Add bananas; microwave, uncovered, on HIGH (100%), about 20 minutes, pausing to stir occasionally, or until jam jells when tested. Continue as for Fruit Salad Jam above.

Each method makes about 1.5 litres (6 cups) of jam.

■ Storage: In a cool, dark place for about 6 months; refrigerate after opening.

APRICOT LEMON PROCESSOR MARMALADE

1 large (300g) orange
2 large (360g) lemons
2 tablespoons water
1²/₃ cups (250g) dried apricots
1.75 litres (7 cups) water, extra
9 cups (2kg) sugar, approximately

Remove and reserve seeds from unpeeled quartered orange and lemons. Put seeds and the 2 tablespoons water in small bowl; cover, set aside. Blend or process chopped orange, lemons and apricots, in batches, until finely chopped; combine fruit with extra water in small boiler or large pan. Bring to boil then simmer, covered, 45 minutes. Transfer mixture to large heatproof bowl, cover. Stand both fruit mixture and seeds, separately, overnight.

Next day, drain seeds over small bowl; reserve liquid, discard seeds. Measure fruit mixture; allow 1 cup (220g) sugar for each cup fruit mixture.

Return fruit mixture and reserved seed liquid to pan; bring to boil. Add sugar; cook, stirring over heat, without boiling, until sugar is dissolved. Bring back to boil; boil rapidly, uncovered, about 30 minutes, stirring occasionally, or until marmalade jells when tested. Stand 5 minutes. Skim surface, pour into hot sterilised jars; seal while hot.

Makes about 2 litres (8 cups).

■ Storage: In a cool, dark place for about 6 months; refrigerate after opening.

MICROWAVE APRICOT LEMON PROCESSOR MARMALADE

This recipe was tested in an 850-watt microwave oven.

1 small (150g) orange
1 large (180g) lemon
1 tablespoon water
3/4 cup (105g) dried apricots
2 cups (500ml) water, extra
3 cups (660g) sugar, approximately

Remove and reserve seeds from unpeeled quartered orange and lemon. Put seeds and the 1 tablespoon water in small bowl; cover, set aside. Blend or process chopped orange, lemon and apricots, in 2 or 3 batches, until finely chopped; combine fruit with extra water in large microwave-safe bowl. Microwave, covered, on HIGH (100%), about 20 minutes, pausing occasionally to stir, or until rind is soft. Do not uncover; stand both fruit mixture and seeds, separately, overnight.

Next day, drain seeds over small bowl; reserve liquid, discard seeds. Measure fruit mixture; allow 1 cup (220g) sugar for each cup fruit mixture. Return fruit mixture, reserved seed liquid and sugar to same bowl; microwave, uncovered, on HIGH (100%) 5 minutes, pausing occasionally to stir sugar until dissolved. Microwave further 5 minutes, without stirring, or until marmalade jells when tested. Stand 5 minutes. Skim surface, pour into hot sterilised jars; seal while hot.

Makes about 3 1/2 cups (875ml).

■ Storage: In a cool, dark place for about 6 months; refrigerate after opening.

OPPOSITE: Fruit Salad Jam.
RIGHT: Apricot Lemon Marmalade.

Jam pot, cup and saucer from Accoutrement; tray from House¹ In Newtown; tiles from Country Floors

TOMATO RELISH

8 medium (1.5kg) tomatoes
3 medium (450g) onions, chopped
1½ cups (300g) firmly packed
brown sugar
1½ cups (375ml) malt vinegar
1½ tablespoons mustard powder
1 tablespoon curry powder
½ teaspoon cayenne pepper
2 teaspoons salt

Peel and roughly chop tomatoes; combine with remaining ingredients in small
boiler or large pan. Cook, stirring over
heat, without boiling, until sugar is dissolved. Bring to boil then simmer immediately, uncovered, about 1¼ hours,
stirring occasionally, or until mixture is
pulpy. Pour mixture into hot sterilised
jars; seal while hot.

Makes about 1 litre (4 cups).

■ Storage: In a cool, dark place for
about 6 months; refrigerate after
opening.
■ Freeze: Not suitable.
■ Microwave: Not suitable.

ABOVE FROM TOP: Beetroot Relish;
Tomato Relish.
OPPOSITE: Uncooked Chilli Sauce.

BEETROOT RELISH

5 large (1kg) beetroot,
peeled, chopped
4 large (800g) onions,
roughly chopped
1 cup (220g) caster sugar
1 tablespoon salt
1 teaspoon ground allspice
2 cups (500ml) malt vinegar
1 tablespoon plain flour

Blend or process beetroot and onions,
in batches, until finely chopped. Combine mixture with sugar, salt, allspice
and 1½ cups (375ml) of the vinegar in
a small boiler or large pan; bring to boil,
boil, uncovered, stirring occasionally,
for 30 minutes. Blend flour with remaining vinegar in small bowl, stir into beetroot mixture; cook, stirring over heat,
until mixture boils and thickens. Pour
into hot sterilised jars; seal while hot.

Makes about 1.75 litres (7 cups).

■ Storage: In a cool, dark place for
about 6 months; refrigerate after
opening.
■ Freeze: Not suitable.
■ Microwave: Not suitable.

UNCOOKED CHILLI SAUCE

It's recommended that you wear
kitchen gloves when handling and
chopping fresh chillies to avoid
irritating your skin. We used Thai
red chillies in this recipe but you can
experiment with others. Use this sauce
as an ingredient in cooking as well
as serving it as a condiment.

250g fresh red chillies
2 tablespoons finely grated
fresh ginger
3 cloves garlic, crushed
1 teaspoon grated lemon rind
¼ cup (50g) firmly packed
brown sugar
½ cup (125ml) white vinegar

Wash chillies; remove and discard
stalks but do not remove membranes
or seeds. Quarter chillies then blend or
process with remaining ingredients
until the consistency of a thick sauce.
Pour chilli mixture into hot sterilised
jars; seal immediately.

Makes about 1½ cups (375ml).

■ Can be made 1 month ahead.
■ Storage: In refrigerator.
■ Freeze: Not suitable.

VINAIGRETTE VARIATIONS

These recipes are tasty variations on the classic French salad dressing. While they are best eaten the same day they are made, they can be kept, refrigerated, up to 3 days. Each recipe makes 1 cup (250ml).

BASIC VINAIGRETTE

1 teaspoon Dijon mustard
1 teaspoon sugar
1/4 cup (60ml) lemon juice
3/4 cup (180ml) olive oil

Combine mustard and sugar in medium bowl; gradually whisk in juice. Add oil, gradually, in a thin stream, whisking constantly. Season with salt and pepper to taste.

ITALIAN-STYLE VINAIGRETTE

1 teaspoon Dijon mustard
1 teaspoon sugar
2 cloves garlic, crushed
1/4 cup (60ml) lemon juice
3/4 cup (180ml) olive oil
2 teaspoons shredded fresh basil

Combine mustard, sugar and garlic in medium bowl; gradually whisk in juice. Add oil, gradually, in a thin stream, whisking constantly. Stir in basil; season with salt and pepper to taste.

MACADAMIA VINAIGRETTE

1 teaspoon Dijon mustard
1 teaspoon sugar
1/4 cup (60ml) lemon juice
1/4 cup (60ml) olive oil
1/2 cup (125ml) macadamia oil

Combine mustard and sugar in medium bowl; gradually whisk in juice. Add combined oils, gradually, in a thin stream, whisking constantly. Season with salt and pepper to taste.

ABOVE FROM LEFT: Basic Vinaigrette, in bowl; Italian-Style Vinaigrette; Macadamia Vinaigrette; Honey Apple Vinaigrette. OPPOSITE FROM TOP: Oven-Dried Capsicums; Oven-Dried Tomatoes.

HONEY APPLE VINAIGRETTE

1 teaspoon Dijon mustard
3 teaspoons honey
2 tablespoons cider vinegar
2 tablespoons apple juice
2/3 cup (160ml) olive oil

Combine mustard and honey in medium bowl; gradually whisk in vinegar and juice. Add oil, gradually, in a thin stream, whisking constantly. Season with salt and pepper to taste.

OVEN-DRIED CAPSICUMS

8 medium (1.6kg) red capsicums
3 medium (600g) yellow capsicums
1 sprig fresh rosemary
1/4 cup loosely packed fresh
   sage leaves
olive oil

Cut off and discard both ends of the capsicums; quarter capsicums lengthways, remove and discard seeds and membranes. Place capsicums, cut-side down, with rosemary and sage, on wire racks set in oven trays. Bake in very slow oven until ingredients are dry; sage will take about 20 minutes, rosemary about 30 minutes, and capsicums about 4 hours. Turn and rearrange capsicums frequently while drying.

Pack capsicums and herbs into hot sterilised jars. Pour in enough oil to cover capsicums completely; seal jars.

- Can be eaten immediately but flavour improves after 3 weeks.
- Storage: In refrigerator for 6 months.
- Freeze: Not suitable.
- Microwave: Not suitable.

OVEN-DRIED TOMATOES

25 medium (2kg) egg tomatoes
1/2 cup loosely packed fresh
   basil leaves
3 (about 10g) fresh
   bird's-eye chillies
3 cloves garlic, sliced
1 tablespoon sea salt
olive oil

Halve tomatoes lengthways; place tomatoes, cut-side up, with basil, chillies and garlic on wire racks set in oven trays. Sprinkle tomatoes with salt. Bake in very slow oven until ingredients are dry; both basil and garlic will take about 2 hours, and tomatoes about 8 hours. Turn and rearrange tomatoes frequently while drying.

Pack tomatoes, basil, chillies and garlic into hot sterilised jars. Pour in enough oil to cover tomatoes completely; seal jars.

- Can be eaten immediately but flavour improves after 3 weeks.
- Storage: In refrigerator for 6 months.
- Freeze: Not suitable.
- Microwave: Not suitable.

PICKLED OLIVES

These will be ready to eat after about 5 weeks sealed in salted water; do not mix green and black varieties of olives when pickling them.

1.5kg fresh black or green olives
⅓ cup (75g) fine sea salt
1 litre (4 cups) water
½ cup (125ml) olive oil, approximately

1. Discard any over-blemished olives. Using a sharp knife, make 2 cuts lengthways in each olive, through to stone.

2. Place olives in 2-litre (8-cup) sterilised jars until jars are two-thirds full; cover olives with cold water. To keep olives submerged, fill a small plastic bag with cold water, tie bag securely, sit on top olives in jar.

3. Scum will appear on surface of water.

4. Change water in jars daily, refilling with fresh, cold water. Change water for 4 days with black olives, for 6 days with green olives.

5. Combine salt and the 1 litre (4 cups) of water in medium pan, stirring over heat until salt is dissolved; cool.

6. Discard water in jars; fill with enough salted water to cover olives.

7. Pour enough oil in jars to cover completely; seal jars.
■ Storage: Sealed, in cool, dark place up to 6 months.
■ Freeze: Not suitable.
■ Microwave: Not suitable.

MARINATED OLIVES

Olives must be pickled before they can be marinated; after being marinated 2 weeks, olives will be ready to eat.

600g drained black or green pickled olives
1 clove garlic, sliced
2 lemon wedges
1 sprig fresh dill
2 cups (500ml) olive oil

Combine olives, garlic, lemon and dill in 1-litre (4-cup) hot sterilised jar; pour oil over top, seal jar.
■ Best made about 2 weeks ahead.
■ Storage: Covered, in cool, dark place up to 2 months.
■ Freeze: Not suitable.

OPPOSITE: Marinated Green and Black Olives.

Bowls and candlesticks from Corso De' Fiori

MARINATED EGGPLANTS

10 (600g) baby eggplants
salt
1 litre (4 cups) white vinegar
2 cups (500ml) water
1 tablespoon chopped fresh mint
1 teaspoon dried thyme leaves
1 clove garlic, finely sliced
1 small fresh red chilli,
  seeded, chopped
1/2 teaspoon ground black pepper
2 cups (500ml) hot olive oil,
  approximately

Quarter eggplants lengthways, place in colander, sprinkle all over with salt; stand 1 hour. Rinse eggplants well under cold water; dry thoroughly.

Heat vinegar, water and 2 teaspoons salt in large pan; do not boil. Add eggplants; simmer, uncovered, 5 minutes. Drain; discard vinegar mixture.

Combine herbs, garlic, chilli, pepper and eggplants in hot sterilised 1-litre (4-cup) jar; pour in enough oil to leave 1cm space between eggplants and top of jar. Seal while hot.

▨ Can be made 1 week ahead.
▨ Storage: In refrigerator for 3 months.
▨ Freeze: Not suitable.
▨ Microwave: Not suitable.

MARINATED ARTICHOKE HEARTS

10 medium (2kg) globe artichokes
3 medium (420g) lemons, halved
1 clove garlic, crushed
1 teaspoon black peppercorns
1 litre (4 cups) white vinegar
2 cups (500ml) water
2 cups (500ml) hot olive oil,
  approximately

Remove and discard stems from each artichoke; snap off and discard tough outer leaves until just centre core of leaves remains. Trim away dark green parts, cut away top of core; rub all over artichokes with 1 lemon half. Place artichokes in large bowl with another lemon half; cover artichokes with water.

Heat garlic, peppercorns, vinegar and the 2 cups of water in large pan; do not boil. Add the drained artichokes and remaining lemon halves; simmer, uncovered, 15 minutes. Drain; discard vinegar mixture and lemon halves. Cool.

Remove and discard centre leaves and chokes with spoon; cut artichoke hearts in half. Place hearts in hot sterilised 1-litre (4-cup) jar; pour in enough oil to leave 1cm space between artichoke hearts and top of jar. Seal while hot.

▨ Can be made 1 week ahead.
▨ Storage: In refrigerator for 3 months.
▨ Freeze: Not suitable.
▨ Microwave: Not suitable.

MARINATED CAPSICUMS

3 medium (600g) red capsicums
3 medium (600g) yellow capsicums
1 litre (4 cups) white vinegar
2 cups (500ml) water
2 teaspoons salt
1 clove garlic, finely sliced
1 teaspoon dried thyme leaves
3 dried bay leaves
1/2 teaspoon ground black pepper
2 cups (500ml) hot olive oil,
  approximately

Cut off and discard both ends of capsicums, remove and discard seeds and membranes; cut capsicums lengthways into 4cm pieces. Heat vinegar, water and salt in large pan; do not boil. Add capsicum pieces; simmer gently, uncovered, 15 minutes. Drain; discard vinegar mixture.

Combine hot capsicum pieces with garlic, both leaves and pepper in hot sterilised 1-litre (4-cup) jar; pour in enough oil to leave 1cm space between capsicum pieces and top of jar. Seal while hot.

▨ Can be made 1 week ahead.
▨ Storage: In refrigerator for 3 months.
▨ Freeze: Not suitable.
▨ Microwave: Not suitable.

MARINATED MUSHROOMS

1 litre (4 cups) white vinegar
2 cups (500ml) water
2 teaspoons salt
800g button mushrooms
1 tablespoon chopped fresh parsley
1 teaspoon dried thyme leaves
1 clove garlic, finely sliced
1/2 teaspoon ground black pepper
2 cups (500ml) hot olive oil,
  approximately

Heat vinegar, water and salt in large pan; do not boil. Add mushrooms; simmer gently, uncovered, 5 minutes. Drain; discard vinegar mixture.

Combine hot mushrooms, herbs, garlic and pepper in hot sterilised 1-litre (4-cup) jar; pour in enough oil to leave 1cm space between mushrooms and top of jar. Seal while hot.

▨ Can be made 1 week ahead.
▨ Storage: In refrigerator for 3 months.
▨ Freeze: Not suitable.
▨ Microwave: Not suitable.

CLOKWISE FROM TOP: Marinated Eggplants; Marinated Artichoke Hearts; Marinated Capsicums; Marinated Mushrooms.

Celebration

Traditional favourites, ready for the happiest of holidays and most special occasions in this cornucopia of mouthwatering guises, are among our most requested recipes, and with good reason: like close friends, they're straightforward and reliable yet also have loads of surprising charm and endearing appeal.

IRISH FRUIT CAKE

2¼ cups (375g) raisins, chopped
2⅓ cups (375g) sultanas, chopped
¼ cup (50g) red glace
    cherries, chopped
¼ cup (50g) green glace
    cherries, chopped
½ cup (85g) dried dates,
    seeded, chopped
⅓ cup (55g) prunes,
    seeded, chopped
¼ cup (55g) chopped
    glace pineapple
⅓ cup (55g) mixed peel
2 teaspoons grated lemon rind
2 teaspoons grated orange rind
2 tablespoons lemon juice
¼ cup (60ml) orange juice
⅓ cup (80ml) Irish whiskey
1 small (130g) apple, peeled, grated
185g butter, softened
¾ cup (165g) caster sugar
3 eggs
½ cup (50g) walnuts,
    toasted, chopped
⅓ cup (40g) ground almonds
1½ cups (225g) plain flour
¼ teaspoon ground nutmeg
½ teaspoon ground cinnamon
2 tablespoons Irish whiskey, extra

Combine fruit, rinds, juices, whiskey and apple in large screw-top jar; shake well. Store jar in cool, dark place for 3 weeks; turn jar daily.

Line the base and side of a deep 20cm round cake pan with 3 thicknesses baking paper, bringing paper 5cm above side of pan.

Beat butter and sugar in medium bowl with electric mixer until just combined; add eggs, 1 at a time, beating well between additions. Place fruit mixture in large bowl; mix in walnuts, ground almonds and egg mixture. Stir in combined sifted flour and spices, spread mixture in prepared pan; decorate with blanched almonds and extra red glace cherries, if desired.

Bake in slow oven 3 hours (cover with foil during cooking if overbrowning). Brush hot cake with extra whiskey; cover, cool in pan.

■ Can be made 3 months ahead.
■ Storage: In airtight container, in refrigerator.
■ Freeze: Suitable.
■ Microwave: Not suitable.

RICH CHRISTMAS PUDDING

You need a 60cm-square piece of unbleached calico to make the pudding cloth for this recipe. If calico has not been used before, soak in cold water overnight; next day, boil it for 20 minutes then rinse under cold water. You can make six small gift puddings from this mixture.

2 cups (340g) chopped raisins
2 cups (320g) dried dates,
    seeded, chopped
½ cup (150g) chopped glace figs
½ cup (125g) chopped
    glace apricots
1 medium (150g) apple,
    peeled, grated
½ cup (125ml) Tia Maria or Kahlua
250g butter, softened
1 teaspoon grated orange rind
1 teaspoon grated lemon rind
1½ cups (300g) firmly packed
    brown sugar
4 eggs
1 cup (150g) plain flour
2 teaspoons mixed spice
½ teaspoon bicarbonate of soda
4 cups (280g) stale breadcrumbs

Mix dried and glace fruit, apple and liqueur in large bowl. Cover, stand overnight or up to a week.

Beat butter, rinds and sugar in small bowl with electric mixer until smooth; beat in eggs, 1 at a time, until just combined between additions. Transfer to large bowl; stir in fruit mixture. Mix in sifted dry ingredients and breadcrumbs, in 2 batches.

Fill large boiler about three-quarters full of water; bring to a rapid boil. Have 2.5 metres of string and ½ cup (75g) plain flour close by. Wearing rubber gloves, dip prepared pudding cloth into boiling water; boil 1 minute then remove, carefully squeezing out excess water.

Working quickly, spread hot cloth on bench, rub flour into centre to cover an area about 40cm in diameter, leaving flour a little thicker in centre of cloth where pudding "skin" should be thickest.

Line medium bowl with cloth, allowing edges to hang over sides; place mixture in centre then gather cloth evenly around pudding, avoiding any deep pleats. Lift pudding out of bowl, pat into round shape; return to bowl, tie cloth tightly with string as close to pudding as possible (tie loop in string to make pudding easier to remove). Pull ends of cloth tightly to ensure pudding is as round and firm as possible. Carefully lower pudding into boiling water; tie free ends of string to handles of boiler to suspend pudding. Cover with tight-fitting lid; boil rapidly about 6 hours, replenishing water as necessary to maintain level.

Untie pudding from handles; place wooden spoon through loop in string to lift pudding from water. Do not place pudding on bench; suspend from spoon by placing over rungs of upturned stool or wedging handle in a drawer. Pudding must be suspended freely. Twist wet ends of cloth around string to avoid them touching pudding. If pudding has been cooked correctly, cloth will start to dry in patches within a few minutes; hang 10 minutes.

Place pudding in large bowl; cut string, carefully peel back cloth. Turn pudding onto a plate, then carefully peel away cloth completely. If pudding is to be served, stand at least 20 minutes or until skin darkens before serving. If pudding is to be stored and reheated for serving later, cool to room temperature. Wrap pudding in plastic wrap then seal tightly in freezer bag or airtight container.

Mini Boiled Puddings: Cut 6 x 40cm squares of unbleached calico; prepare, as above, using ¼ cup (35g) plain flour for each cloth. Divide mixture evenly among cloths; tie each pudding as above. Boil rapidly 2 hours. Remove the 6 mini puddings from water; cool and store as for boiled pudding.

To Reheat: Thaw frozen pudding(s) 3 days in refrigerator; remove from refrigerator 12 hours before reheating.

Remove plastic wrap; tie dry, unfloured cloth around pudding(s). Boil 1 hour for mini puddings, 2 hours for one large pudding, following instructions above. Hang hot pudding(s) 10 minutes. Remove cloth; stand at least 20 minutes or until skin darkens before serving.

To Heat in Microwave Oven: Reheat up to 4 single serves at once. Cover with plastic wrap; microwave on HIGH (100%) up to 1 minute per serve. To reheat whole pudding, cover with plastic wrap; microwave on MEDIUM (50%) about 15 minutes or until hot.

▨ Storage: In freezer bag or airtight container in refrigerator for up to 2 months.
▨ Freeze: Suitable up to 12 months.
▨ Microwave: Suitable for reheating.

STEAMED CHRISTMAS PUDDING

2¾ cups (500g) mixed dried fruit
¾ cup (120g) dried dates,
    seeded, chopped
¾ cup (120g) raisins, chopped
1 cup (250ml) water
½ cup (110g) caster sugar
½ cup (100g) firmly packed
    brown sugar
125g butter
1 teaspoon bicarbonate of soda
2 eggs, lightly beaten
1 cup (150g) plain flour
1 cup (150g) self-raising flour
1 teaspoon mixed spice
½ teaspoon ground cinnamon
2 tablespoons rum

Grease 2.25-litre (9-cup) pudding basin, line base with baking paper.

Combine the fruit, water, sugars and butter in medium pan; stir over heat until butter is melted and sugars are dissolved. Bring to boil then immediately simmer, uncovered, 8 minutes. Remove from heat, stir in soda; cool.

Stir in eggs, sifted dry ingredients and rum; spoon mixture into prepared basin, cover with baking paper then foil, secure with lid or string. Place pudding basin in large pan or boiler with enough boiling water to come halfway up side; cover with tight-fitting lid. Boil 5 hours, adding more water if necessary. Stand 15 minutes before turning out.

▨ Can be made 1 month ahead.
▨ Storage: Covered, in refrigerator.
▨ Freeze: Suitable.
▨ Microwave: Not suitable.

OPPOSITE FROM TOP: Rich Christmas Pudding; Steamed Christmas Pudding.

TRADITIONAL ROAST TURKEY WITH MIX-AND-MATCH SEASONINGS

4kg turkey
1 tablespoon vegetable oil
1/4 cup (35g) plain flour
2 teaspoons chicken stock powder
2 cups (500ml) water

Discard neck and giblets from turkey. Rinse turkey under cold water; pat dry inside and out. Tuck wings under body; spoon seasoning loosely into cavity. Tuck trimmed neck flap under body, securing with toothpicks or small skewers; tie legs together with string.

Place turkey on greased wire rack in a flameproof baking dish with a little water in it; brush turkey evenly with oil. Bake, uncovered, in moderate oven, brushing occasionally with oil, about 2 1/2 hours or until tender; cover breast with greased foil if overbrowning.

Remove turkey from dish, cover with foil. Leave 1 1/2 tablespoons of pan juices in dish; discard remainder or reserve for another use. Place dish on heat, stir in flour; cook, stirring, until lightly browned. Remove from heat, gradually stir in combined stock powder and water; return to heat, stir until gravy boils and thickens. Strain into serving jug.

Serves 8 to 10.

■ Best made on day of serving.
■ Storage: Covered, in refrigerator.
■ Freeze: Not suitable.
■ Microwave: Not suitable.

SAGE AND ONION SEASONING

20g butter
1 medium (150g) onion, chopped
2 sticks celery, chopped
3 bacon rashers, chopped
300g sausage mince
2 1/2 cups (175g) stale breadcrumbs
1 tablespoon chopped fresh sage
1/3 cup (35g) ground hazelnuts
2 eggs, lightly beaten

Heat butter in medium pan; cook onion, celery and bacon, stirring, until onion is soft. Stir in mince; cook, stirring, until it just changes colour; cool. Mix in remaining ingredients.

FIG AND MARMALADE SEASONING

1/3 cup (65g) chopped dried figs
1 tablespoon Grand Marnier or orange juice
2 teaspoons vegetable oil
1 small (80g) onion, finely chopped
1 large (200g) apple, finely chopped
2 bacon rashers, finely chopped
1 1/2 cups (105g) stale breadcrumbs
2 tablespoons orange marmalade
1 egg, lightly beaten
2 tablespoons chopped fresh parsley
2 teaspoons chopped fresh thyme

Combine figs and liqueur in small bowl; stand 20 minutes.

Heat oil in small pan; cook onion, apple and bacon, stirring, until onion is soft. Transfer mixture to large bowl; stir in fig mixture, breadcrumbs, marmalade, egg and herbs.

HAZELNUT AND HERB SEASONING

60g butter
1 large (200g) onion, chopped
1 clove garlic, crushed
1/2 cup (75g) roasted hazelnuts, chopped
2 tablespoons chopped fresh basil
1 tablespoon chopped fresh parsley
1 tablespoon chopped fresh oregano
2 tablespoons cranberry sauce
2 eggs, lightly beaten
1/2 teaspoon seasoned pepper
4 cups stale breadcrumbs

Heat butter in small pan; cook onion and garlic, stirring, until onion is soft. Transfer mixture to large bowl; stir in remaining ingredients.

FRUITY SEASONING

2 teaspoons vegetable oil
1 medium (150g) onion, chopped
4 cups (280g) stale breadcrumbs
1 cup (150g) chopped dried apricots
1 cup (170g) chopped raisins
1 tablespoon chopped fresh thyme
2 tablespoons mint jelly
2 tablespoons brandy
1 egg, lightly beaten

Heat oil in small pan; cook onion, stirring, until soft. Transfer to large bowl, stir in remaining ingredients.

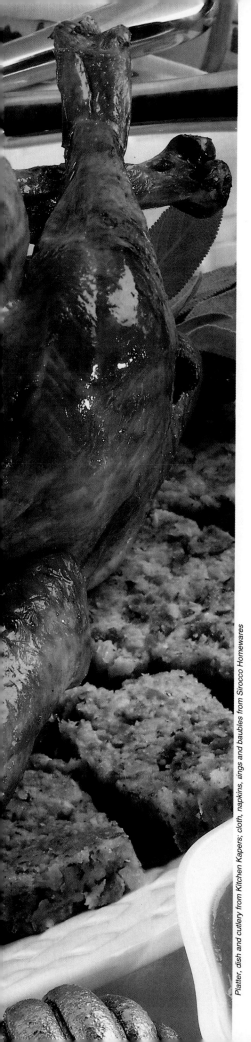

Platter, dish and cutlery from Kitchen Kapers; cloth, napkins, icings and baubles from Sirocco Homewares

LEFT: Traditional Roast Turkey; Sage and Onion Seasoning.

SHORTBREAD

125g unsalted butter, softened
¼ cup (55g) caster sugar
1 cup (150g) plain flour
¼ cup (35g) rice flour or ground rice

Grease a 19cm x 29cm rectangular slice pan.

Beat butter and sugar in small bowl with electric mixer until just combined; gradually beat in the combined sifted flours, in about 6 batches, mixing between additions.

Knead dough into a ball on floured surface; press dough evenly into the prepared pan.

Using a knife, mark dough lengthways into 6 strips, each about 3cm wide; prick evenly all over with a fork.

Bake in slow oven about 40 minutes or until golden brown. Remove from oven, cut into finger lengths. Stand shortbread 10 minutes; turn onto wire rack to cool.

■ Can be made up to 1 month ahead.
■ Storage: Covered, in airtight container.
■ Freeze: Suitable.
■ Microwave: Not suitable.

PECAN CANDY CAKES

1½ cups (315g) red and green glace cherries, halved
¾ cup (165g) coarsely chopped glace pineapple
1½ cups (250g) dried dates, seeded, chopped
1 tablespoon self-raising flour
3½ cups (350g) pecans
1¾ cups (115g) shredded coconut
400g can sweetened condensed milk

Grease two 8cm x 26cm bar pans, line base and sides with baking paper.

Combine all ingredients in large bowl, mix well; press into prepared pans.

Bake in slow oven about 1 hour or until firm. Cool. Remove cakes from pans, wrap in plastic wrap; refrigerate overnight or until required.

■ Can be made 2 weeks ahead.
■ Storage: Covered, in refrigerator.
■ Freeze: Not suitable.
■ Microwave: Not suitable.

OPPOSITE: Shortbread.
RIGHT: Pecan Candy Cakes.

TRUFFLE TREE

The tree shown here is a charming help-yourself centrepiece decorated for the Christmas table with melt-in-the-mouth truffles. The tree will hold about 80 truffles: double any one of the recipes below to fill the tree with a single variety; halve each of the following recipes to decorate with an assortment of truffles. Each truffle recipe can be made up to a month before required and stored under refrigeration in an airtight container; none can be frozen.

2kg bag cement powder
30cm piece wood dowelling
25cm diameter shallow terracotta flower pot
1 large polystyrene ball (about 39cm in circumference)
gold paint
Christmas decorations
thick toothpicks

Mix enough cement to anchor dowelling in centre of flower pot for strength and stability; allow to set thoroughly. Paint pot and dowelling with gold paint; dry completely.

Arrange Christmas decorations over dried cement; gently push ball onto top of dowelling.

Insert 1 toothpick into each truffle. Start inserting truffles in a ring around widest part of ball's circumference; this ensures rows of truffles will be straight and even at top and bottom of ball. Refrigerate Truffle Tree until required.

HONEY IRISH CREAM TRUFFLES

1 cup (100g) sweet biscuit crumbs
½ cup (45g) desiccated coconut
¼ cup (40g) sultanas, chopped
½ cup (80g) icing sugar mixture
1 tablespoon cocoa powder
¼ cup (60ml) Irish cream liqueur
1 tablespoon water
1 tablespoon honey
⅓ cup (35g) chocolate sprinkles, approximately

Combine crumbs, coconut, sultanas, sugar and sifted cocoa in medium bowl. Stir in liqueur, water and honey. Roll rounded teaspoons of mixture into balls; roll balls in chocolate sprinkles. Place in single layer on tray; refrigerate truffles about 4 hours or until firm.

Makes about 30.

CHOCOLATE AND GRAND MARNIER TRUFFLES

You can substitute any orange flavoured liqueur for the Grand Marnier.

½ cup (125g) glace apricots, finely chopped
2 tablespoons Grand Marnier
150g dark cooking chocolate, melted
1½ cups (150g) chocolate cake crumbs
¼ cup (25g) cocoa powder, approximately

Combine apricots and liqueur in small bowl; stand 30 minutes. Combine chocolate and crumbs in medium bowl; stir in apricot mixture. Refrigerate until firm. Roll rounded teaspoons of mixture into balls, place in single layer on tray; refrigerate truffles about 4 hours or until firm.

Just before inserting toothpicks, roll truffles in sifted cocoa.

Makes about 35.

HAZELNUT AND IRISH CREAM TRUFFLES

½ cup (125ml) cream
250g dark chocolate, finely chopped
3 teaspoons Irish cream liqueur
⅓ cup (40g) finely chopped roasted hazelnuts
250g dark chocolate Melts, melted

Bring cream to boil in small pan; pour over dark chocolate in small bowl, stirring until chocolate melts. Stir in liqueur and nuts. Cover; refrigerate, stirring occasionally, about 30 minutes or until mixture starts to thicken but does not set. Roll rounded teaspoons of mixture into balls, place in single layer on tray; refrigerate truffles until firm.

Dip truffles in Melts then quickly and gently roll between palms to coat evenly. Return to tray; refrigerate about 4 hours or until firm.

Makes about 35.

BRANDIED PEACH TRUFFLES

¼ cup (60ml) cream
30g butter
250g white chocolate Melts, chopped
½ cup (125g) finely chopped glace peaches
3 teaspoons brandy
½ cup (45g) desiccated coconut, approximately

Bring cream and butter to boil in small pan; remove from heat, add Melts, stirring until melted. Stir in peaches and brandy. Cover; refrigerate, stirring occasionally, about 30 minutes or until mixture starts to thicken but does not set. Roll rounded teaspoons of mixture into balls. Place in single layer on tray; refrigerate truffles about 4 hours or until firm.

Just before inserting toothpicks, roll truffles in coconut.

Makes about 40.

LIME AND MALIBU TRUFFLES

¼ cup (60ml) cream
30g butter
250g white chocolate Melts, chopped
2 teaspoons grated lime rind
2 teaspoons Malibu
250g white chocolate Melts, melted, extra

Bring cream and butter to boil in small pan; add Melts in small bowl, stirring until they are melted. Stir in rind and Malibu. Cover; refrigerate, stirring occasionally, about 30 minutes or until mixture starts to thicken but does not set. Roll rounded teaspoons of mixture into balls, place in single layer on tray; refrigerate truffles until firm. Dip truffles in extra melted Melts then quickly and gently roll between palms to coat evenly. Return to tray; refrigerate about 4 hours or until firm.

Makes about 35.

Silver strawberry-shaped dishes from The Pacific East India Company; silver artichoke and Christmas decorations from Home & Garden on the Mall; Glasses from Bohemia Crystal Shop

GLAZED HAM

Most people prefer buying a cooked leg of ham and glazing it themselves about an hour before serving time. All of the following glazes can be made up to a week before using and stored, covered, in the refrigerator; none is suitable to freeze. Ham itself can be frozen for up to 8 weeks but should be glazed just before baking.

8kg cooked leg of ham
whole cloves

Make a decorative cut through ham rind about 10cm from shank end of leg; run thumb under edge of rind at other end of leg then, using fingers to loosen it, pull rind away from the fat. Continue to carefully pull rind away from fat until you reach decorative cut at shank end; discard rind.

Make shallow cuts in one direction diagonally across fat at 2cm intervals then shallow cut diagonally in opposite direction, forming diamonds. Do not cut through surface of top fat or fat will spread, losing pattern, during cooking. Place 1 clove in centre of each diamond then position ham on wire rack in large baking dish. Wrap shank with foil; brush ham with glaze.

Bake, uncovered, in moderate oven about 50 minutes or until browned all over, brushing frequently with glaze during cooking.

MAPLE SYRUP GLAZE

1 tablespoon mustard powder
1½ cups (375ml) maple-
**   flavoured syrup**
⅓ cup (80ml) cider vinegar

Mix all ingredients in small bowl until powder dissolves.

REDCURRANT JELLY AND ORANGE GLAZE

½ cup (125ml) redcurrant jelly
¼ cup (60ml) port
½ cup (125ml) orange juice
½ cup (125ml) marmalade

Mix all ingredients in small pan; stir over low heat until jelly and marmalade melt. Simmer 5 minutes or until mixture thickens slightly.

MANGO GLAZE

⅔ cup (160ml) mango nectar
⅓ cup (80ml) mango chutney
¼ cup (50g) firmly packed
**   brown sugar**
1 tablespoon Dijon mustard

Mix all ingredients in small pan; stir over low heat until chutney melts.

APRICOT GLAZE

⅔ cup (160ml) apricot nectar
⅓ cup (80ml) apricot jam
¼ cup (50g) firmly packed
**   brown sugar**
1 tablespoon Dijon mustard

Mix all ingredients in small pan; stir over low heat until jam melts.

SWEET CHILLI GLAZE

⅓ cup (80ml) mild sweet chilli sauce
¼ cup (60ml) lime juice
2 teaspoons finely grated
**   fresh ginger**
2 tablespoons teriyaki sauce

Mix all ingredients in small bowl.

BARBECUE HONEY GLAZE

¼ cup (60ml) barbecue sauce
¼ cup (60ml) Worcestershire sauce
¼ cup (60ml) tomato sauce
¼ cup (60ml) honey

Mix all ingredients in small pan; stir over low heat until honey melts.

CLOCKWISE FROM TOP: Redcurrant Jelly and Orange Glaze; Apricot Glaze; Barbecue Honey Glaze; Mango Glaze. CENTRE: Sweet Chilli Glaze.

FESTIVE FRUIT AND NUT CAKE

This cake will be easier to cut if it has been refrigerated.

2 glace pineapple rings
1/2 cup (125g) glace apricots
1 1/2 cups (250g) Brazil nuts
1 1/2 cups (250g) dried dates, seeded
2/3 cup (140g) red glace cherries
2/3 cup (140g) green glace cherries
3/4 cup (120g) whole
    blanched almonds
2 eggs
1/2 cup (100g) firmly packed
    brown sugar
2 teaspoons vanilla essence
1 tablespoon rum
90g butter, softened
1/3 cup (50g) plain flour
1/4 cup (35g) self-raising flour

Grease 14cm x 21cm loaf pan, line base and sides with baking paper.

Chop pineapple and apricots into pieces equal in size to Brazil nuts; leave remaining fruit and nuts whole. Combine all fruit and nuts in large bowl. Beat eggs in small bowl with electric mixer until thick and creamy; beat in sugar, essence, rum and butter then stir into fruit mixture. Mix in with combined sifted flours; spread mixture into prepared pan.

Bake in slow oven about 2 hours or until firm. Cover hot cake with foil; cool. Remove cake from pan, wrap in plastic wrap; refrigerate until required.

■ Can be made 3 months ahead.
■ Storage: Airtight container, in refrigerator.
■ Freeze: Not suitable.
■ Microwave: Not suitable.

BELOW: Festive Fruit and Nut Cake.
OPPOSITE: Super-Rich Chocolate Drambuie Fruit Cake.

SUPER-RICH CHOCOLATE DRAMBUIE FRUIT CAKE

We made this quantity of mixture into one deep 22cm round cake and six "Texas-style" muffin-size (3/4 cup/180ml) individual cakes. If you prefer, you can make a larger cake by using a deep 25cm round or deep 23cm square cake pan; allow about 4 to 4 1/2 hours for baking.

2 1/3 cups (375g) sultanas
2 1/4 cups (375g) raisins, chopped
1 2/3 cups (250g) currants
1 1/2 cups (300g) prunes,
    seeded, chopped
1 1/2 cups (250g) dried dates,
    seeded, chopped
3/4 cup (125g) mixed peel
2/3 cup (140g) red glace
    cherries, quartered
1 1/3 cups (330ml) Drambuie
1/3 cup (80ml) honey
1 tablespoon grated lemon rind
250g butter
1 1/2 cups (300g) firmly packed
    dark brown sugar
6 eggs
90g dark chocolate, grated
1 1/4 cups (125g) pecans, chopped
2 cups (300g) plain flour
1 cup (150g) self-raising flour
1/4 cup (25g) cocoa powder

Grease 6-hole (3/4 cup/180ml) Texas-style muffin pan; grease then line base and side of deep 22cm round or deep 19cm square cake pan with 3 thicknesses baking paper, bringing paper 5cm above edge of pan.

Mix fruit, 1 cup (250ml) of the Drambuie, honey and rind in large bowl. Cover; stand overnight or several days.

Beat butter and sugar in medium bowl with electric mixer until just combined. Add eggs, 1 at a time, beating until combined between additions. Stir into fruit mixture with chocolate and nuts. Stir in combined sifted dry ingredients, in 2 batches.

Fill, level to the top, each hole of prepared muffin pan with mixture; spread remaining mixture into prepared cake pan. Decorate tops with extra pecans and glace cherries, if desired.

Bake muffins in very slow oven 1 1/2 hours (cake can stand while muffins are baking). Brush hot muffins with some of the remaining Drambuie; cover with foil, cool in pan. Bake large cake in slow oven 3 hours. Brush hot cake with remaining Drambuie; cover with foil, cool in pan.

- Can be made 3 months ahead.
- Storage: Covered, in refrigerator.
- Freeze: Suitable.
- Microwave: Not suitable.

Glasses from Orson & Blake Collectables; cake stand from Kitchen Kapers; square plate from Accoutrement

GINGERBREAD JUMBLES HOUSE

We used Arnott's Honey Jumbles for the gingerbread house. You also need a piece of board measuring at least 50cm x 55cm, a large piece of thick cardboard, masking tape, cotton wool and your choice of decorations. The house can be assembled 2 weeks ahead and kept, airtight, in a cool, dry place.

6 x 125g packets Honey Jumbles
6 x 200g packets pink musk sticks
icing sugar mixture

FROSTING
1¼ cups (275g) caster sugar
½ cup (125ml) water
3 egg whites

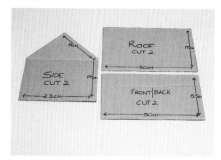

1. Using the measurements shown in this photograph as a guide, cut cardboard patterns for the house.

2. Cover the board (measuring at least 50cm x 55cm) with foil. Assemble house with masking tape; secure to board with tape.

3. Spread a layer of frosting on front wall of house; attach Honey Jumbles in a brick pattern, cutting Honey Jumbles where necessary to allow for a window and door. Repeat with both side walls, allowing space for a window on each wall. Cover the entire back wall with Honey Jumbles.

4. Cut a few musk sticks into thin strips; use to represent window frames and panes. Use trimmed musk sticks to represent door.

Spread frosting on roof. Attach two rows of overlapping musk sticks on roof; top roof with musk sticks.

Trim Honey Jumbles into chimney shape to fit slope of roof; attach them to roof with frosting. Similarly, attach a small piece of cotton wool to chimney to represent smoke.

Dust gingerbread house with sifted icing sugar; decorate garden as desired.
Frosting: Combine sugar and water in pan; stir over heat, without boiling, until sugar is dissolved. Boil, uncovered, 3 to 5 minutes or until sugar syrup is slightly thickened but not coloured (115°C on candy thermometer). Syrup can be tested by dropping 1 teaspoon into cup of cold water; it should form a soft ball when gathered and rolled gently between the fingers.

Beat egg whites in medium bowl with electric mixer until firm peaks form. Pour hot syrup in thin stream onto egg whites with mixer operating on medium speed. Continue beating until frosting stands in firm peaks.

AUSTRALIAN CHRISTMAS PUDDING

½ cup (125g) finely chopped
   glace apricots
½ cup (125g) finely chopped
   glace peaches
2 tablespoons (35g) finely chopped
   red glace cherries
2 tablespoons (35g) finely chopped
   green glace cherries
¼ cup (40g) sultanas
¼ cup (60ml) brandy
2 teaspoons gelatine
1 tablespoon water
4 eggs, separated
½ cup (80g) icing sugar mixture
¼ cup (25g) cocoa powder
60g dark chocolate, melted
⅓ cup (50g) hazelnuts, chopped
50g chocolate-coated honeycomb
   bar, chopped
300ml thickened cream
100g white chocolate Melts, melted

Combine fruit and brandy in large bowl; cover, stand overnight.

Line 1.375-litre (5½-cup) pudding basin with plastic wrap.

Sprinkle gelatine over water in cup, stand in pan of simmering water, stir until dissolved; cool.

Beat egg whites in medium bowl with electric mixer until firm peaks form; gradually beat in sifted combined icing sugar and cocoa. Fold in lightly beaten egg yolks and cooled chocolate.

Stir gelatine mixture, hazelnuts and honeycomb into fruit mixture; fold in chocolate mixture. Beat cream in small bowl until soft peaks form; fold into fruit mixture. Pour mixture into prepared pudding basin; cover, freeze several hours or overnight.

Just before serving, turn pudding onto serving plate; smooth surface with wet hands. Spoon white chocolate over the top.

Serves 8.

■ Must be made a day ahead.
■ Storage: Covered, in freezer, for up to a week.
■ Microwave: Gelatine and chocolate suitable.

FROZEN CHESTNUT PUDDING

We used a French product labelled Chestnut Spread; some cans may be labelled Sweetened Chestnut Puree but as long as the French translation is Creme de Marrons, you will be using the correct ingredient for this recipe, one made of pureed chestnuts, candied chestnut pieces, sugar, glucose syrup and vanilla. Cans labelled simply Chesnut Puree are not suitable because the content consists only of processed chestnuts and water.

½ cup (85g) raisins, chopped
⅓ cup (70g) red glace
   cherries, chopped
3 (100g) glace apricots, chopped
6 (30g) dried dates, seeded, chopped
¼ cup (60ml) dark rum
3 eggs
⅓ cup (75g) caster sugar
¾ cup (250g) canned
   chestnut spread
600ml thickened cream

Combine fruit and rum in small bowl; cover, stand overnight.

Line 1.375-litre (5½-cup) pudding basin with plastic wrap.

Whisk eggs and sugar in medium bowl over pan of simmering water until slightly thickened; stir in chestnut spread. Cool.

Beat cream in small bowl with electric mixer until soft peaks form; fold into chestnut mixture. Stir in undrained fruit mixture. Pour mixture into prepared pudding basin; cover, freeze several hours or overnight.

Just before serving, turn pudding onto serving plate; smooth surface with wet hands.

Serves 8.

■ Must be made a day ahead.
■ Storage: Covered, in freezer, for up to a week.
■ Microwave: Not suitable

China from Villeroy & Boch; tray and pineapple from The Parterre Garden

LEFT: Australian Christmas Pudding; Frozen Chestnut Pudding.

ECONOMICAL STEAMED PUDDING

2 pot-strength tea bags (about 1 tablespoon/6g loose tea)
1 cup (250ml) boiling water
2 cups (375g) mixed dried fruit
1 cup (200g) firmly packed brown sugar
1 egg, lightly beaten
2 cups (300g) self-raising flour
1 teaspoon ground cinnamon
1 teaspoon ground nutmeg

Grease 1.5-litre (6-cup) pudding basin, line base with baking paper.

Combine tea bags (or loose tea) and water in jug; stand for 5 minutes. Discard tea bags (strain loose tea); cool. Combine fruit and tea in large bowl; cover, stand overnight.

Mix in remaining ingredients; spoon mixture into prepared basin. Cover with baking paper then foil, secure with lid or string. Place pudding basin in large pan with enough boiling water to come halfway up side; cover. Boil 3 hours, adding more water if necessary. Stand 5 minutes before turning out.

Serves 8.

■ Can be made a month ahead.
■ Storage: Covered, in refrigerator.
▓ Microwave: Not suitable.
▓ Freeze: Suitable.

ECONOMICAL FRUIT CAKE

4 cups (750g) mixed dried fruit
185g butter
1 cup (200g) firmly packed brown sugar
1/3 cup (80ml) sweet sherry or orange juice
1 tablespoon instant coffee powder
1/2 teaspoon bicarbonate of soda
3 eggs, lightly beaten
1 1/2 cups (225g) plain flour
1 tablespoon mixed spice

Line base and side of deep 20cm round cake pan with 3 thicknesses baking paper, bringing paper 5cm above edge of pan.

Combine fruit, butter, sugar, sherry and coffee powder in large pan; stir over heat until butter is melted and sugar dissolved. Cover; simmer 5 minutes. Remove from heat, stir in soda. Transfer fruit mixture to large bowl; cool.

Mix eggs, and sifted flour and spice, into fruit mixture; spread evenly into prepared pan, decorate top with blanched almonds, if desired.

Bake in slow oven 2 1/2 hours. Cover hot cake with foil; cool in pan.

■ Can be made a month ahead.
■ Storage: Covered, in airtight container, in refrigerator.
▓ Freeze: Suitable.
▓ Microwave: Not suitable.

FROM TOP: Economical Fruit Cake; Economical Steamed Pudding.

Plates from Waterford Wedgwood; tins from Home & Garden on the Mall

GRAND MARNIER FRUIT CAKE

This is one of our more extravagant recipes. The dried fruit is soaked for 10 days in the orange-flavoured liqueur, giving the cake its deliciously special taste.

3 cups (500g) sultanas
1½ cups (250g) mixed peel
¾ cup (120g) chopped raisins
¾ cup (120g) chopped seeded dried dates
⅔ cup (140g) chopped seeded prunes
½ cup (125g) chopped glace apricots
⅔ cup (150g) chopped glace pineapple
½ cup (70g) slivered almonds
½ cup (60g) chopped walnuts
1 tablespoon grated orange rind
½ cup (110g) caster sugar
¼ cup (60ml) orange juice
½ cup (125ml) Grand Marnier
250g butter, softened
½ cup (100g) firmly packed brown sugar
5 eggs
2 cups (300g) plain flour
2 tablespoons Grand Marnier, extra

Combine all fruit in jar or large container having tight-fitting lid; mix in almonds, walnuts and rind.

Sprinkle caster sugar evenly into heavy-based large pan. Cook, over low heat, without stirring, until sugar begins to melt; at that point, immediately begin stirring until sugar is completely melted and golden brown. Remove from heat, stir in orange juice. Return to heat, stirring constantly until toffee-like pieces have dissolved. Do not boil or mixture will evaporate. Stir in liqueur then strain into jug; discard any small pieces of toffee. Pour over fruit mixture; cover tightly with plastic wrap or lid.

Next day, turn jar upside down or stir fruit well; do this daily for 10 days.

The day of baking cake, line deep 19cm square or deep 22cm round cake pan with 4 thicknesses baking paper, bringing paper 5cm above edge of pan.

Beat butter and brown sugar in medium bowl with electric mixer until combined; add eggs, 1 at a time, beating until just combined between additions. Pour fruit mixture into large bowl; add egg mixture, mix with hand. Add sifted flour, mix well with hand then spread mixture into prepared pan. Bake in slow oven 3½ hours. Brush extra liqueur over top, leave cake in pan, cover hot cake with foil. Wrap in towel; cool overnight. Do not remove lining paper if storing cake.

■ Can be made 6 months ahead.
■ Storage: Airtight container, in refrigerator.
■ Freeze: Suitable.
■ Microwave: Not suitable.

ABOVE: Grand Marnier Fruit Cake.
RIGHT: Last-Minute Fruit Cake.

LAST-MINUTE FRUIT CAKE

2⅓ cups (375g) sultanas
1½ cups (250g) raisins, chopped
1⅔ cups (250g) currants
¾ cup (125g) mixed peel
½ cup (100g) glace cherries, halved
¼ cup (55g) chopped
   glace pineapple
¼ cup (60g) chopped glace apricots
250g butter
1 cup (200g) firmly packed
   brown sugar
½ cup (125ml) brandy
½ cup (125ml) water

2 teaspoons grated orange rind
1 teaspoon grated lemon rind
1 tablespoon treacle
5 eggs, lightly beaten
1¾ cups (255g) plain flour
⅓ cup (50g) self-raising flour
½ teaspoon bicarbonate of soda

Line base and sides deep 19cm square or deep 22cm round cake pan with 3 thicknesses baking paper, bringing paper 5cm above edge of pan.

Combine fruit, butter, sugar, brandy and water in pan; stir over heat until butter is melted and sugar is dissolved.

Bring to boil then immediately remove from heat. Transfer mixture to large bowl; cool.

Stir in the rinds, treacle and eggs, then the sifted dry ingredients. Spread mixture evenly into prepared pan.

Bake in slow oven 2½ hours. Cover hot cake in pan with foil; cool.

▨ Can be made up to 3 months ahead.
▨ Storage: Airtight container, in refrigerator.
▨ Freeze: Suitable.
▨ Microwave: Not suitable.

Glasses and Christmas decorations from Home & Garden on the Mall; compote from Bohemia Crystal Shop; box and tray from The Pacific East India Company

THREE-IN-ONE CHRISTMAS MIX

One quantity of this Basic Fruit Mixture recipe makes enough for all three of the Christmas recipes pictured here. The mixture should be made a month before required and stored in a cool, dark place – the refrigerator is ideal. Grand Marnier liqueur was used in keeping with the citrus content of the mixture but you can substitute it with rum, sherry or brandy, if desired.

BASIC FRUIT MIXTURE

Any type of jam can be used.

6 cups (1kg) sultanas
2½ cups (375g) currants
2¼ cups (375g) raisins, chopped
1½ cups (250g) dried dates,
   seeded, chopped
1½ cups (250g) prunes,
   seeded, chopped
1¼ cups (250g) glace
   cherries, quartered
½ cup (125g) glace
   apricots, chopped
½ cup (115g) chopped
   glace pineapple
½ cup (115g) glace ginger, chopped
¾ cup (125g) mixed peel
3 medium (450g) apples,
   peeled, grated
⅔ cup (160ml) fig jam
2 tablespoons grated orange rind
¼ cup (60ml) lemon juice
2 cups (500g) firmly packed
   brown sugar
1 tablespoon mixed spice
1⅓ cups (330ml) Grand Marnier

Mix all ingredients in large bowl. Cover tightly with plastic wrap. Store the mixture in a cool, dark place for a month (or longer, if desired) before using; stir mixture every 2 or 3 days.

MOIST CHRISTMAS CAKE

½ quantity Basic Fruit Mixture
250g butter, melted, cooled
5 eggs, lightly beaten
2½ cups (375g) plain flour
2 tablespoons Grand Marnier

Line base and sides of deep 19cm square or deep 22cm round cake pan with 2 thicknesses brown paper and 2 thicknesses baking paper, bringing paper 5cm above edge of pan.

Place Basic Fruit Mixture in large bowl. Mix in butter, eggs and sifted flour, in batches. Spread mixture into prepared pan, level top with spatula; decorate with blanched almonds and cherries, if desired. Bake in slow oven 4 hours. Brush with liqueur, cover hot cake in pan with foil; cool.

■ Can be made 3 months ahead.
■ Storage: Airtight container, in refrigerator.
■ Freeze: Suitable.
■ Microwave: Butter suitable.

CHRISTMAS PUDDING

You need a 60cm-square piece of unbleached calico to make the pudding cloth. If calico has not been used before, soak in cold water overnight; next day, boil it for 20 minutes then rinse under cold water.

¼ quantity Basic Fruit Mixture
250g butter, melted, cooled
3 eggs, lightly beaten
4 cups (280g) stale breadcrumbs
¼ cup (35g) plain flour

Mix all ingredients in large bowl.

Fill a large boiler three-quarters full of water; bring to rapid boil. Have ready 2.5 metres of string and ½ cup (75g) plain flour. Wearing rubber gloves, dip prepared pudding cloth in boiling water; boil 1 minute then remove, carefully squeeze excess water from cloth. Working quickly, spread hot cloth on bench, rub flour into centre to cover an area about 40cm in diameter, leaving flour a little thicker in centre of cloth where "skin" on the pudding needs to be thickest.

Line medium bowl with the cloth, allowing edges to hang over sides; place mixture in centre. Gather cloth evenly around pudding, avoiding any deep pleats. Lift pudding out of bowl, pat into round shape; return to bowl. Tie cloth tightly with string as close to pudding as possible (tie loop in string to make pudding easier to remove). Pull ends of cloth tightly to ensure pudding is as round and firm as possible.

Carefully lower pudding into boiling water; tie free ends of string to handles of boiler to suspend pudding. Cover with tight-fitting lid; boil rapidly for 4 hours, replenishing water as necessary to maintain level.

Untie pudding from handles; place wooden spoon through loop in string to lift pudding from water. Do not put pudding on bench; suspend from spoon by placing over rungs of upturned stool or wedging handle in a drawer. Pudding must be suspended freely. Twist wet ends of cloth around string to avoid them touching pudding. If pudding has been cooked correctly, cloth will start to dry in patches within a few minutes; hang 10 minutes.

Place pudding in large bowl; cut string, carefully peel back cloth. Turn pudding onto a plate, then carefully peel cloth away completely; cool. Stand at least 20 minutes or until skin darkens before serving.

To Store: Wrap pudding in plastic wrap then seal tightly in freezer bag or airtight container.

To Reheat: Thaw frozen pudding 3 days in refrigerator; remove from refrigerator 12 hours before reheating.

Remove plastic wrap; tie dry, unfloured cloth around pudding. Boil 2 hours, following instructions above.

China from Waterford Wedgwood; box from The Pacific East India Company

Hang hot pudding 10 minutes. Remove cloth; stand at least 20 minutes or until skin darkens before serving.

To Reheat in Microwave Oven: Reheat up to 4 single serves at once. Cover with plastic wrap; microwave on HIGH (100%) up to 1 minute per serve. To reheat whole pudding, cover with plastic wrap; microwave on MEDIUM (50%) about 15 minutes or until hot.

■ Storage: In refrigerator, up to 2 months.
■ Freeze: Suitable, up to 12 months.
■ Microwave: Butter suitable.

FRUIT MINCE TARTS

Using a quarter of the Basic Fruit Mixture, this recipe makes about 48 bite-size tarts.

1 cup (150g) plain flour
1 cup (150g) self-raising flour
½ cup (75g) cornflour
¼ cup (30g) custard powder
¼ cup (40g) icing sugar mixture
250g cold butter, chopped
¼ cup (60ml) iced water,
    approximately
¼ quantity Basic Fruit Mixture

Sift dry ingredients into bowl, rub in butter; mix in only enough water so ingredients just cling together. Knead on floured surface until smooth. Divide pastry into 4 pieces, wrap in plastic wrap; refrigerate 30 minutes.

Roll 1 piece pastry between 2 sheets baking paper to 2mm thickness; cut pastry into 7cm rounds. Put rounds in holes of patty-pan tray; fill each with 1 level tablespoon Basic Fruit Mixture. Decorate with pastry scraps.

Bake in moderate oven 15 to 20 minutes. Stand 5 minutes; cool on wire rack. Repeat process with remaining pastry and mixture.

Makes about 48.
■ Can be made 2 days ahead.
■ Storage: Airtight container.
■ Freeze: Uncooked pastry suitable.
■ Microwave: Not suitable.

CLOCKWISE FROM TOP LEFT: Moist Christmas Cake; Christmas Pudding; Fruit Mince Tarts.

THE AUSTRALIAN WOMEN'S WEEKLY FRUIT CAKE

The most popular of all of our fruit cakes, this traditional stand-by keeps and cuts well – so it can double as a spectacular wedding cake too! Sherry or brandy can be substituted for rum if preferred.

3 cups (500g) sultanas
1½ cups (250g) raisins, chopped
²/₃ cup (140g) red glace
 cherries, quartered
¾ cup (125g) dried currants
¾ cup (125g) mixed peel
2 tablespoons marmalade
½ cup (125ml) rum
250g butter, softened
1 teaspoon grated orange rind
1 teaspoon grated lemon rind
1 cup (200g) firmly packed
 brown sugar
4 eggs
2 cups (300g) plain flour
2 teaspoons mixed spice
1 cup (160g) blanched almonds,
 approximately
2 tablespoons rum, extra

Line base and sides of deep 19cm square or deep 22cm round cake pan with 3 thicknesses baking paper, bringing paper 5cm above edge of pan.

Mix fruit, marmalade and rum in large bowl. Beat butter, rinds and sugar in small bowl with electric mixer until just combined; beat in eggs, 1 at a time, until just combined between additions. Stir butter mixture into fruit mixture; mix in sifted flour and spice. Spread mixture into the prepared pan, decorate with blanched almonds.

Bake in slow oven 3½ hours. Brush extra rum over top, cover hot cake, in pan, with foil; cool.

■ Can be made 3 months ahead.
■ Storage: Covered, in refrigerator.
■ Freeze: Suitable.
■ Microwave: Not suitable.

HOT CROSS BUNS

**1 tablespoon (2 sachets/14g)
  dry yeast**
1/4 cup (55g) caster sugar
1 cup (250ml) milk, warmed
4 cups (600g) plain flour
1 teaspoon ground cinnamon
1/2 teaspoon mixed spice
60g butter, chopped
1 egg, lightly beaten
1/2 cup (125ml) warm water
3/4 cup (125g) dried currants
1/4 cup (40g) mixed peel
1 tablespoon apricot jam

FLOUR PASTE
1/2 cup (75g) plain flour
1 tablespoon caster sugar
1/3 cup (80ml) warm water

Grease 23cm square slab pan.

Combine yeast, sugar and milk in small bowl; stir until yeast is dissolved. Cover bowl, stand in warm place for about 15 minutes or until yeast mixture is frothy.

Sift flour and spices into large bowl; rub in butter. Stir in yeast mixture, egg, water, currants and peel; cover, stand in warm place about 1 hour or until mixture has doubled in size.

Turn dough onto floured surface; knead until smooth and elastic. Divide dough into pieces; knead into bun shapes. Place in prepared pan, cover loosely with greased plastic wrap; stand in warm place 20 minutes or until buns almost double in size.

Place flour paste in piping bag fitted with small plain tube; pipe crosses onto tops of risen buns. Bake in moderately hot oven 10 minutes; reduce heat to moderate, bake 15 minutes. Turn buns onto wire rack; brush with warmed sieved jam.

Flour Paste: Combine flour and sugar in small bowl; gradually blend in water, stir until smooth.

Makes 16.

■ Best made on day of serving.
■ Storage: In airtight container.
■ Freeze: Suitable.
■ Microwave: Not suitable.

OPPOSITE: The Australian Women's Weekly Fruit Cake.
RIGHT: Hot Cross Buns.

Platter, butter dish and napkins from Kitchen Kapers; chenille throw from Sirocco Homewares

SIMNEL CAKE

250g butter, softened
1 tablespoon finely grated
   lemon rind
1 cup (200g) firmly packed
   brown sugar
½ cup (110g) caster sugar
4 eggs
½ cup (100g) glace cherries, halved
1½ cups (250g) sultanas
1½ cups (250g) raisins, chopped
1½ cups (250g) mixed peel
½ cup (50g) walnuts, chopped
⅓ cup (55g) blanched
   almonds, chopped
½ cup (125ml) sweet sherry
3 cups (450g) plain flour
1 teaspoon mixed spice
1 tablespoon apricot jam

ALMOND PASTE
3 cups (375g) ground almonds
1½ cups (330g) caster sugar
1 egg, beaten
few drops almond essence
1 teaspoon lemon juice,
   approximately

FONDANT GLAZE
1 cup (220g) caster sugar
½ cup (125ml) water
pinch cream of tartar
2½ cups (400g) pure icing sugar,
   approximately
red and green food colouring

Line base and side of deep 22cm round cake pan with 2 thicknesses brown paper and 2 thicknesses baking paper, bringing paper 5cm above edge of pan.

Beat butter, rind and sugars in medium bowl with electric mixer until just combined; add eggs, 1 at a time, beating well between additions. Transfer mixture to large bowl; mix in fruit, peel, nuts, sherry, and sifted flour and spice. Spread half of the cake mixture into prepared pan. Roll a third of the almond paste into a 22cm circle; carefully place on top cake mixture in pan, spread with remaining cake mixture.

Bake in slow oven 3¼ hours or until cooked when tested. Cover hot cake with foil; cool in pan.

Roll 12 x ½ teaspoons almond paste into egg shapes. Using a fork, dip 4 egg shapes in green fondant glaze, shake gently to remove excess; dry on wire rack. Repeat with remaining egg shapes, stirring fondant glaze over bowl of hot water to thin, if necessary; dip 4 in pink fondant glaze and 4 in white fondant glaze.

Roll remaining almond paste into a 22cm circle. Brush cake with warmed sieved jam; carefully place almond paste circle on top cake, flute edges with fingers.

Spread remaining white fondant glaze in cake centre to within 2.5cm of edge; decorate with eggs.

Almond Paste: Combine almonds and sugar in medium bowl; stir in egg, essence and enough juice to make a firm paste.

Fondant Glaze: Combine caster sugar, water and cream of tartar in pan; stir over heat, without boiling, until sugar is dissolved. Simmer, uncovered, without stirring, 3 minutes; cool.

Just before use, stir enough sifted icing sugar into mixture to result in a thick, coating consistency.

Divide fondant glaze among 3 small bowls; colour one quantity pale green, colour a second quantity pale pink, and leave remaining quantity white.

■ Can be made 1 month ahead.
■ Storage: Covered, in refrigerator.
■ Freeze: Suitable.
■ Microwave: Not suitable.

Plates from Kitchen Kapers; cake stand from The Home Store; chenille throw from Sirocco Homewares

Cake pan sizes

Use the chart shown at right as a guide for the correct cake pan size. If using an unusual cake pan shape (oval, hexagonal or similar), there is a simple method of determining how much cake mixture you require. Fill a deep 19cm-square or deep 22cm-round cake pan with water and pour this water into the unusual-shaped pan: each full pan of water represents a 250g (½lb) quantity of fruit cake mixture.

Preparing the oven

■ As a guide, the top of the cake should be in the centre of the oven.

■ If baking more than one cake at a time, check that cake pans will fit by arranging them, empty, in a cold oven. The cake pans should not touch each other, or the oven wall or door, to allow for even circulation of heat.

■ Cakes on different racks should be changed about halfway through cooking time – move the lower cakes to the top rack and vice versa.

■ When cooking more than one cake on a rack, best results will be obtained if you change their positions in the oven halfway through cooking time, to ensure even browning.

Lining the pan

■ To ensure a perfect-shaped cake, pans must be lined correctly. Lining paper protects the cake during long cooking: the longer the cooking time, the heavier the lining paper should be.

■ To line sides, cut 1 strip of brown paper and 2 to 3 strips of greaseproof or baking paper long enough to fit around the pan and about 8cm wider than the depth of the pan. Put baking paper strips on top of the brown paper strip; fold lengthways about 2cm from edge and make diagonal cuts about 2cm apart up to the fold. Fit prepared strip around the curves or corners of the cake pan, with the brown paper pressed against the pan and the cut section resting on the base.

Fruit Cakes

Before you start making a fruit cake, read the following tips for perfect results.

■ Staple or pin the 2 ends of the strip of paper together so they do not curl or separate before cake mixture is added.

■ The pans do not need greasing; however, if paper is not fitting snugly against the edge of pan, a small amount of butter or cooking oil spray will help hold it together.

■ Using base of pan as a guide, cut 3 paper shapes to cover base; position over cut edge of strip lining the side.

Making the cake

■ Using scissors, cut raisins the same size as sultanas, quarter the cherries.

■ Combine sultanas, raisins, currants, mixed peel, cherries, rind and rum; mix well then cover securely. Mixture can be stored up to 7 days at this stage.

■ It is important to have the eggs and butter at room temperature.

■ Beat butter only until it just clings to side of the bowl; add sugar, beat only until just combined – overcreaming the butter and sugar could result in a crumbly cake.

■ Add fruit mixture to creamed mixture; mix ingredients together with your hand.

■ Mix in sifted flour and spice.

■ Drop small amounts of mixture into corners of prepared pan to weight paper lining, holding paper in position, if necessary, to keep it from slipping.

- Spread remaining mixture firmly into prepared pan; smooth top with spatula or damp hand.

- Drop pan firmly onto bench from a height of about 15cm to settle mixture in the pan.

- If desired, a rich fruit cake mixture can be prepared ahead, placed in the prepared pan, its surface covered with a piece of greaseproof paper or plastic food wrap, then refrigerated for up to a week. Allow the cake to come to room temperature before baking.

To test if cake is cooked

- After minimum specified cooking time, feel top of cake with fingertips.

- If cake feels firm, gently push a thin sharp knife (eg, a vegetable knife) into the centre of the cake, right through to base of pan. Gently withdraw the knife and feel the blade: if it is simply sticky from fruit, the cake is cooked; if there is moist cake mixture on the blade, return the cake to the oven for a further 15 minutes before testing again.

When cake is cooked

- Make cuts in lining paper level with top of the pan then fold paper down over the surface of the cake. Cover the hot cake tightly with foil, completely wrap cake tightly in a towel; cool cake as is, in pan.

To store

- After about 12 hours, when cake is completely cold, remove from the pan. Leaving lining paper intact, wrap cake completely in plastic wrap.

- Place wrapped cake in an airtight container or plastic freezer bag. Store in a cool place or, if weather is humid, refrigerate up to 6 months; cake can be frozen up to 12 months.

- If the cake is to be decorated, it is a good idea to cool it upside down on a flat surface. This will give the cake a flat top. Do not wrap the cake in a towel if cooling this way.

FRUIT CAKE CHART

Ingredients	125g (¹/₄lb) Mixture	250g (¹/₂lb) Mixture	375g (³/₄lb) Mixture	500g (1lb) Mixture	625g (1¹/₄lb) Mixture	750g (1¹/₂lb) Mixture
Sultanas	375g	750g	1kg	1.125kg	1.75kg	2kg
Raisins	125g	250g	375g	500g	625g	750g
Currants	60g	125g	185g	250g	315g	375g
Mixed Peel	60g	125g	185g	250g	315g	375g
Glace Cherries	60g	125g	185g	250g	315g	375g
Grated Orange Rind	¹/₂ teaspoon	1 teaspoon	1 teaspoon	2 teaspoons	2 teaspoons	3 teaspoons
Grated Lemon Rind	¹/₂ teaspoon	1 teaspoon	1 teaspoon	2 teaspoons	2 teaspoons	3 teaspoons
Rum, Brandy or Sherry	¹/₄ cup	¹/₂ cup	³/₄ cup	1 cup	1¹/₄ cups	1¹/₂ cups
Butter	125g	250g	375g	500g	625g	750g
Brown Sugar	¹/₂ cup	1 cup	1¹/₂ cups	2 cups	2¹/₂ cups	3 cups
Eggs (large, 60g)	2	4	6	8	10	12
Marmalade	1 tablespoon	2 tablespoons	¹/₄ cup	¹/₃ cup	5 tablespoons	¹/₂ cup
Plain Flour	1 cup	2 cups	3 cups	4 cups	5 cups	6 cups
Mixed Spice	¹/₂ teaspoon	1 teaspoon	1¹/₂ teaspoons	2 teaspoons	2¹/₂ teaspoons	3 teaspoons
Square Cake Pan	15cm	19cm	23cm	25cm	28cm	30cm
Round Cake Pan	17cm	22cm	25cm	28cm	30cm	33cm
Approximate Cooking Time	2¹/₂ to 3 hours	3 to 3¹/₂ hours	4 to 4¹/₂ hours	4¹/₂ to 5 hours	5 to 6 hours	6 to 7 hours

NOTE: 1 cup firmly packed brown sugar = 200g
1 cup flour = 150g
4 teaspoons = 1 tablespoon

The recipe in this chart is based on our highly prized Australian Women's Weekly Fruit Cake; while proportions may vary, the ingredients remain consistent with those used in this most popular fruit cake.

Oregano

Rosemary

Chocol
Melt

Curly parsley

Dill

Thyme

Choc Bits

English spinach

Green onions

Lemon grass

Glossary

Here are some terms, names and alternatives to help everyone use and understand our recipes perfectly.

Bay leaves

Sage

Basil

Coriander

Globe artichoke

ALLSPICE: also known as Jamaican pepper or pimento; available whole or ground, tastes like blended cinnamon, clove and nutmeg.

ALMONDS:

Blanched: skins removed.

Flaked: paper-thin slices.

Ground: also known as almond meal.

Slivered: small lengthways-cut pieces.

BACON RASHERS: also known as slices of bacon; made of cured and smoked pork side.

BAKING PAPER: also known as parchment, silicon paper or non-stick baking paper; not to be confused with greaseproof or wax(ed) paper. Used to line pans and to be made into disposable piping bags.

BAKING POWDER: a raising agent consisting mainly of 2 parts cream of tartar to 1 part bicarbonate of soda (baking soda).

BARBECUE SAUCE: a spicy, tomato-based sauce used to marinade and baste, or as an accompaniment to meat and poultry.

BEAN SPROUTS: also known as bean shoots; new growths of beans and seeds germinated for consumption. The most common are mung bean, soy bean, alfalfa and snow pea sprouts.

BEEF:

Boneless sirloin roast: trimmed, flavoursome cut from the sirloin; when sliced, also known as New York cut.

Minced: also known as ground beef.

BEER, LIGHT ALE: an unhopped, low-kilojoule, low-alcohol, English-style beer.

BICARBONATE OF SODA: also known as baking soda.

BISCUIT CRUMBS: crushed, plain biscuits (cookies); available packaged or made at home in a food processor or blender.

BISCUITS: also known as cookies.

Choc-crunch: a plain, hard, uniced, packaged, chocolate biscuit.

Golliwog: a plain, buttery-smooth, uniced, packaged, chocolate biscuit.

Honey Jumbles: an iced, honey and ginger flavoured, cake-like, packaged biscuit.

Milk coffee: an uniced, plain, packaged biscuit, sweetened with golden syrup.

Nice: an uniced, plain, sweet, packaged biscuit, sprinkled with sugar on top.

Sponge-Finger: also known as Savoiardi, Savoy biscuits or ladyfingers; Italian-style crisp biscuits made of a sponge-cake mixture.

BLACK BEAN SAUCE: made from fermented soy beans, spices, water and wheat flour.

BRAN:

Flakes: trade name of a Kellogg's breakfast cereal based on processed wheat bran enriched with 4 vitamins, including folate.

Unprocessed: made from a grain's outer layer, most often the husk of wheat, rice or oats.

BREADCRUMBS:

Packaged: fine-textured, crunchy, purchased, white breadcrumbs.

Stale: one- or two-day-old bread made into crumbs by grating, blending or processing.

BUTTER: salted or unsalted ("sweet") butter; 125g is equal to 1 stick butter.

BUTTERMILK: low-fat milk cultured with bacteria to give it a slightly sour, tangy taste; low-fat yogurt can be substituted.

CAJUN SEASONING: a packaged blend of paprika, basil, onion, fennel, thyme, cayenne and white pepper.

CAPSICUM: also known as bell pepper or, simply, pepper. Seeds and membranes should be discarded before use.

CAYENNE PEPPER: a thin-fleshed, long, extremely hot, red chilli; usually purchased dried and ground.

CHEESE:

Bocconcini: small rounds of fresh "baby" mozzarella, traditionally made in Italy from buffalo milk. Spoils rapidly so must be refrigerated, in brine, for a maximum of 2 days.

Cream: commonly known as "Philadelphia" or "Philly", a soft milk cheese having no less than 33% butterfat.

Fetta: Greek in origin; a crumbly goat's or sheep's milk cheese with a sharp, salty taste.

Light cream: a version of Philadelphia having 30% less fat; used frequently in cooking. Another version is light spreadable Philadelphia, a blend of cottage and cream cheese with 80% less fat than butter; used frequently as a spread for bread.

Mascarpone: a fresh, thick cream cheese with a delicately sweet, slightly sour taste.

Mozzarella: a semi-soft cheese with a

Ginger

Ground ginger

Beetroot

Galangal

Glace ginger

Dried chilli flakes

Fresh red serrano chilli

Bran Flakes

Cracked wheat

Green split peas

delicate, fresh taste; has a low melting point and stringy texture when heated.

Parmesan: a sharp-tasting, dry, hard cheese, made from skim or part-skim milk and aged for at least a year before being sold.

Ricotta: a sweet, fairly moist, fresh curd cheese having a low fat content.

Tasty: matured cheddar; use an aged, hard, pronounced-flavoured variety.

CHESTNUT SPREAD: also known as Sweetened Chestnut Puree or Creme de Marrons; a French product made of pureed chestnuts, candied chestnut pieces, sugar, glucose syrup and vanilla. Available from good delicatessens; not to be confused with Chestnut Puree, made only of pureed chestnuts and water.

CHILLIES: available in many different types and sizes, used fresh and dried. Rubber gloves should be used when seeding and chopping fresh chillies to avoid burning your skin. Removing seeds and membranes decreases the heat level.

Flakes: crushed dried chillies.

Sweet chilli sauce: a comparatively mild, Thai-type, commercial sauce made from red chillies, sugar, garlic and vinegar.

CHOCOLATE:

Choc Bits: also known as chocolate chips and chocolate morsels; available in milk, white and dark chocolate. Made of cocoa liquor, cocoa butter, sugar and emulsifiers, these hold their shape in baking and are ideal for decorating.

Dark Cooking: we used premium-quality, dark cooking chocolate rather than compound.

Melts: available in milk, white and dark chocolate. Made of sugar, vegetable fats, milk solids, cocoa powder, butter oil and emulsifiers, these are good for melting and moulding.

Sprinkles: also known as cake tops; tiny pellet-shaped pieces of compounded chocolate used for decorating.

COCONUT:

Cream: available in cans and cartons; made from coconut and water.

Desiccated: unsweetened, concentrated, dried, shredded coconut.

Flaked: dried, flaked coconut flesh.

Milk: pure, unsweetened coconut milk available in cans.

Shredded: thin strips of dried coconut.

CORN CHIPS: packaged snack food that evolved from fried corn tortilla pieces.

CORNFLOUR: also known as cornstarch.

CRACKED WHEAT: whole wheat berries broken during milling into a cereal product of varying degrees of coarseness; used extensively in breadmaking and Middle-Eastern cooking.

CRANBERRY SAUCE: a packaged product made of cooked cranberries in sugar syrup; its astringent flavour goes well with roast poultry.

CREAM:

Fresh (minimum fat content 35%): also known as pure cream and pouring cream; has no additives like commercially-thickened cream.

Sour (minimum fat content 35%): a thick, commercially-cultured soured cream.

Thickened (minimum fat content 35%): a whipping cream containing a thickener.

CREAM OF TARTAR: the acid ingredient in baking powder; added to confectionery mixtures to help prevent sugar crystallising. Keeps frostings creamy and improves volume when beating egg whites.

CURRY POWDER: a blend of ground, powdered spices used for convenience when making Indian food. Can consist of some or all of the following in varying proportions: dried chilli, cinnamon, coriander, cumin, fennel, fenugreek, mace, cardamom and turmeric.

CUSTARD POWDER: packaged, vanilla pudding mixture.

DRIED CURRANTS: tiny, black raisins so-named after the Corinth, Greece, grape.

DRIED MIXED HERBS: a blend of dried, crushed thyme, rosemary, marjoram, basil, oregano and sage.

EGGPLANT: also known as aubergine.

ENGLISH SPINACH: true spinach (the green vegetable often called spinach is correctly silverbeet) with delicate, crinkled, green leaves on thin stems. High in iron, it's best cooked only until just wilted.

ESSENCES: also known as extracts; generally the byproduct of distillation of plants.

FISH SAUCE: also called nam pla or nuoc nam; made from pulverised, salted, fermented fish, most often anchovies. Use sparingly.

FIVE-SPICE POWDER: a fragrant mixture of ground cinnamon, cloves, star anise, Sichuan pepper and fennel seeds.

FLOUR:

Plain: an all-purpose flour, made from wheat.

Rice: very fine flour, made of ground, white rice.

Self-raising: plain flour sifted with baking powder in the proportion of 1 cup flour to 2 teaspoons baking powder.

Wholemeal plain: also known as all-purpose wholewheat flour; has no baking powder.

FOOD COLOURINGS: available in liquid, powder and concentrated paste forms.

FRENCH ONION SOUP MIX: a packaged soup mix often added to meat and poultry dishes for flavour and as a thickening agent.

GALANGAL: also known as laos; this dried root is a member of the ginger family. Used whole or ground, is piquant and peppery.

GINGER:

Fresh: also known as green or root ginger; the thick, gnarled root of a tropical plant used extensively in Asian cooking. Can be kept, peeled, covered with dry sherry in a jar and refrigerated, or frozen in an airtight container.

Glace: fresh ginger root preserved in sugar syrup. Crystallised ginger can be substituted if rinsed with warm water and dried before using.

Ground: also known as powdered ginger; used as a flavouring in cakes, pies and puddings but cannot be substituted for fresh ginger.

GLUCOSE SYRUP: also known as liquid glucose; a sugary syrup obtained from starches such as wheat and corn. Used in confectionery making to avoid crystallisation.

GOLDEN SYRUP: a byproduct of refined sugarcane; substitute with pure maple syrup.

GREEN SPLIT PEAS: also known as field peas; green or yellow pulse grown especially for drying. Used in soups, stews and, occasionally, spiced and cooked on their own.

HERBS: when specified, we used 1 teaspoon dried (not ground) herbs as being the equivalent of 4 teaspoons (1 tablespoon) chopped fresh herbs.

HORSERADISH RELISH: made from seasonal root vegetables, horseradish oil and vinegar; used as an accompaniment to roast and grilled meats.

INSTANT LASAGNE: wide, flat sheets of precooked durum wheat pasta ready to be assembled, with no need for boiling in water.

IRISH WHISKEY: The Irish were the first to make whiskey; theirs is light and dry, made of distilled fermented barley and other grains.

JAM: also known as preserve or conserve; most often made from fruit.

KAFFIR LIME LEAVES: aromatic leaves of a small citrus tree bearing a wrinkled-skinned, yellow-green fruit originally grown in South Africa and Southeast Asia. Used fresh or dried in many Asian dishes.

KUMARA: orange-fleshed sweet potato.

LEMON GRASS: a tall, clumping, lemon-smelling and tasting, sharp-edged grass; the white lower part is used in cooking or for tea.

LIQUEURS:

Drambuie: honey- and herb-flavoured blended Scotch whiskies.

Grand Marnier: orange-flavoured liqueur based on Cognac-brandy.

Irish Cream: we used Baileys Original, based on Irish whiskey, spirits and cream.

Kahlua: coffee-flavoured liqueur.

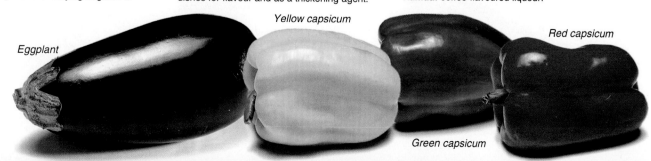

Eggplant

Yellow capsicum

Red capsicum

Green capsicum

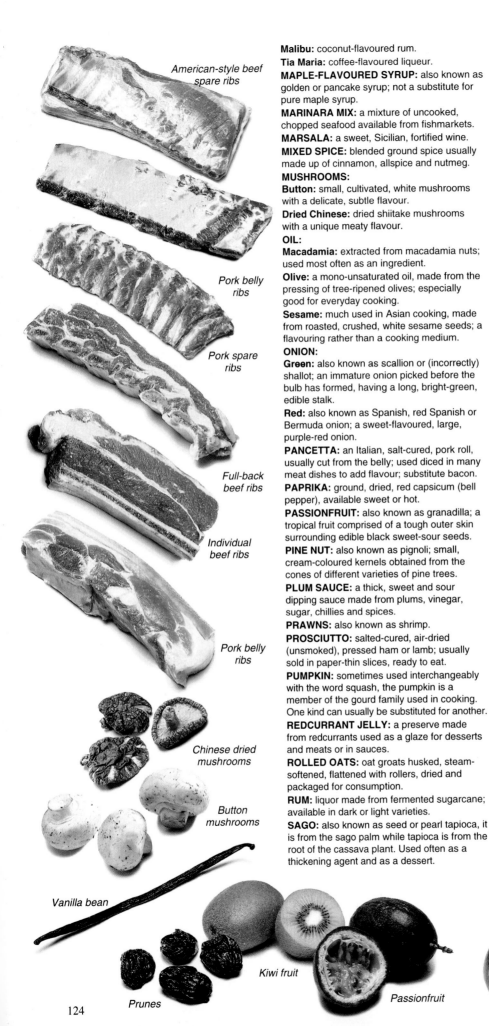

American-style beef spare ribs

Pork belly ribs

Pork spare ribs

Full-back beef ribs

Individual beef ribs

Pork belly ribs

Chinese dried mushrooms

Button mushrooms

Vanilla bean

Prunes

Kiwi fruit

Passionfruit

Red onion

Butternut pumpkin

Malibu: coconut-flavoured rum.

Tia Maria: coffee-flavoured liqueur.

MAPLE-FLAVOURED SYRUP: also known as golden or pancake syrup; not a substitute for pure maple syrup.

MARINARA MIX: a mixture of uncooked, chopped seafood available from fishmarkets.

MARSALA: a sweet, Sicilian, fortified wine.

MIXED SPICE: blended ground spice usually made up of cinnamon, allspice and nutmeg.

MUSHROOMS:

Button: small, cultivated, white mushrooms with a delicate, subtle flavour.

Dried Chinese: dried shiitake mushrooms with a unique meaty flavour.

OIL:

Macadamia: extracted from macadamia nuts; used most often as an ingredient.

Olive: a mono-unsaturated oil, made from the pressing of tree-ripened olives; especially good for everyday cooking.

Sesame: much used in Asian cooking, made from roasted, crushed, white sesame seeds; a flavouring rather than a cooking medium.

ONION:

Green: also known as scallion or (incorrectly) shallot; an immature onion picked before the bulb has formed, having a long, bright-green, edible stalk.

Red: also known as Spanish, red Spanish or Bermuda onion; a sweet-flavoured, large, purple-red onion.

PANCETTA: an Italian, salt-cured, pork roll, usually cut from the belly; used diced in many meat dishes to add flavour; substitute bacon.

PAPRIKA: ground, dried, red capsicum (bell pepper), available sweet or hot.

PASSIONFRUIT: also known as granadilla; a tropical fruit comprised of a tough outer skin surrounding edible black sweet-sour seeds.

PINE NUT: also known as pignoli; small, cream-coloured kernels obtained from the cones of different varieties of pine trees.

PLUM SAUCE: a thick, sweet and sour dipping sauce made from plums, vinegar, sugar, chillies and spices.

PRAWNS: also known as shrimp.

PROSCIUTTO: salted-cured, air-dried (unsmoked), pressed ham or lamb; usually sold in paper-thin slices, ready to eat.

PUMPKIN: sometimes used interchangeably with the word squash, the pumpkin is a member of the gourd family used in cooking. One kind can usually be substituted for another.

REDCURRANT JELLY: a preserve made from redcurrants used as a glaze for desserts and meats or in sauces.

ROLLED OATS: oat groats husked, steam-softened, flattened with rollers, dried and packaged for consumption.

RUM: liquor made from fermented sugarcane; available in dark or light varieties.

SAGO: also known as seed or pearl tapioca, it is from the sago palm while tapioca is from the root of the cassava plant. Used often as a thickening agent and as a dessert.

SAMBAL OELEK (also ulek or olek): Indonesian in origin; a salty paste made from ground chillies.

SAUSAGE MINCE: ground pork or other meat mixed with fat, salt and various seasonings, and sold without the sausage casing; used for meatloaf and terrines.

SHRIMP PASTE: also known as trasi and blanchan; a strong-scented, almost solid, preserved paste made of salted dried shrimp. Used as a pungent flavouring in many Southeast Asian soups and sauces.

SUGAR: we used coarse, granulated table sugar, also known as crystal sugar, unless otherwise specified.

Brown: a soft, fine, granulated sugar containing molasses to give its characteristic colour.

Caster: also known as superfine or finely-granulated table sugar.

Icing sugar mixture: also known as confectioners' sugar or powdered sugar; granulated sugar crushed together with a small amount (about 3%) cornflour.

SULTANAS: golden raisins.

SUNFLOWER SEED KERNELS: from dried, husked sunflower seeds.

TACO SEASONING MIX: a packaged, Mexican seasoning mix made from oregano, cumin, chillies and various other spices.

TERIYAKI SAUCE: a homemade or commercially-bottled sauce usually made from soy sauce, mirin, sugar, ginger and other spices; it imparts a distinctive glaze when brushed on meat to be grilled.

TOMATO:

Paste: triple-concentrated tomato puree used to flavour soups, stews and sauces.

Sauce: also known as ketchup or catsup; a flavoured condiment based on tomatoes, vinegar and spices.

TORTILLA: thin, round, unleavened bread originating in Mexico; can be made at home or purchased frozen, fresh or vacuum-packed. Two kinds are available, one made from wheat flour and the other from corn (maizemeal).

TREACLE: thick, dark syrup not unlike molasses; a byproduct from sugar refining.

VANILLA BEAN: dried long, thin pod from a tropical golden orchid grown in Tahiti, Central and South America; the minuscule black seeds inside the bean are used to impart a luscious vanilla flavour in baking and desserts.

VINEGAR:

Balsamic: authentic only from the province of Modena, Italy; made from a regional wine of white Trebbiano grapes specially processed then aged in antique wooden casks to give its exquisite pungent flavour.

Rice wine: made from fermented rice.

WINE: the adage that you should never cook with wine you wouldn't drink holds true with our books: we always use good-quality dry white and red wines in our recipes.

YEAST: a 7g (¼oz) sachet of dried yeast (2 teaspoons) is equal to 15g (½oz) of compressed yeast.

ZUCCHINI: also known as courgette.

Index

Make your own stock

These stock recipes can be made up to 4 days ahead and stored, covered, in the refrigerator. Be sure to remove any fat from the surface after the cooled stock has been refrigerated overnight. If the stock is to be kept longer, it is best to freeze it in smaller quantities. Stock is also available in cans or tetra packs. Stock cubes or powder can be used. As a guide, 1 teaspoon of stock powder or 1 small crumbled stock cube mixed with 1 cup (250ml) water will give a fairly strong stock. You should be aware of the salt and fat content of stock cubes, powders and prepared stocks.

Fish Stock

1.5kg fish bones
3 litres (12 cups) water
1 medium (150g) onion, chopped
2 sticks celery, chopped
2 bay leaves
1 teaspoon black peppercorns

Combine all ingredients in large pan; simmer, uncovered, 20 minutes. Strain.

Chicken Stock

2kg chicken bones
2 medium (300g) onions, chopped
2 sticks celery, chopped
2 medium (250g) carrots, chopped
3 bay leaves
2 teaspoons black peppercorns
5 litres (20 cups) water

Combine all ingredients in large pan; simmer, uncovered, 2 hours. Strain.

Beef Stock

2kg meaty beef bones
2 medium (300g) onions
2 sticks celery, chopped
2 medium (250g) carrots, chopped
3 bay leaves
2 teaspoons black peppercorns
5 litres (20 cups) water
3 litres (12 cups) water, extra

Place bones and unpeeled chopped onions in baking dish. Bake in hot oven about 1 hour or until bones and onions are well browned. Transfer bones and onions to large pan; add celery, carrots, bay leaves, peppercorns and the water. Simmer, uncovered, 3 hours. Add the extra water; simmer, uncovered, further 1 hour. Strain.

Vegetable Stock

2 large (360g) carrots, chopped
2 large (360g) parsnips, chopped
4 medium (600g) onions, chopped
12 sticks celery, chopped
4 bay leaves
2 teaspoons black peppercorns
6 litres (24 cups) water

Combine all ingredients in large pan; simmer, uncovered, 1½ hours. Strain.

All stock recipes make about 2.5 litres (10 cups).

QUICK CONVERSION GUIDE

Wherever you live in the world you can use our recipes with the help of our easy-to-follow conversions for all your cooking needs. These conversions are approximate only. The difference between the exact and approximate conversion of liquid and dry measures amounts to only a teaspoon or two, and will not make any difference to your cooking results.

MEASURING EQUIPMENT

The difference between measuring cups internationally is minimal within 2 or 3 teaspoons' difference. (For the record, 1 Australian metric measuring cup will hold approximately 250ml.) The most accurate way of measuring dry ingredients is to weigh them. When measuring liquids use a clear glass or plastic jug with the metric markings.

If you would like the measuring cups and spoons as used in our Test Kitchen, turn to page 128 for details and order coupon. In this book we use metric measuring cups and spoons approved by Standards Australia.

● a graduated set of four cups for measuring dry ingredients; the sizes are marked on the cups.
● a graduated set of four spoons for measuring dry and liquid ingredients; the amounts are marked on the spoons.
● 1 TEASPOON: 5ml.
● 1 TABLESPOON:20ml.

NOTE: NZ, CANADA, USA AND UK ALL USE 15ml TABLESPOONS.
ALL CUP AND SPOON MEASUREMENTS ARE LEVEL.

DRY MEASURES

METRIC	IMPERIAL
15g	1/2oz
30g	1oz
60g	2oz
90g	3oz
125g	4oz (1/4lb)
155g	5oz
185g	6oz
220g	7oz
250g	8oz (1/2lb)
280g	9oz
315g	10oz
345g	11oz
375g	12oz (3/4lb)
410g	13oz
440g	14oz
470g	15oz
500g	16oz (1lb)
750g	24oz (11/2lb)
1kg	32oz (2lb)

LIQUID MEASURES

METRIC	IMPERIAL
30ml	1 fluid oz
60ml	2 fluid oz
100ml	3 fluid oz
125ml	4 fluid oz
150ml	5 fluid oz (1/4 pint/1 gill)
190ml	6 fluid oz
250ml	8 fluid oz
300ml	10 fluid oz (1/2 pint)
500ml	16 fluid oz
600ml	20 fluid oz (1 pint)
1000ml (1 litre)	13/4 pints

WE USE LARGE EGGS WITH AN AVERAGE WEIGHT OF 60g

HELPFUL MEASURES

METRIC	IMPERIAL
3mm	1/8in
6mm	1/4in
1cm	1/2in
2cm	3/4in
2.5cm	1in
5cm	2in
6cm	21/2in
8cm	3in
10cm	4in
13cm	5in
15cm	6in
18cm	7in
20cm	8in
23cm	9in
25cm	10in
28cm	11in
30cm	12in (1ft)

HOW TO MEASURE

When using the graduated metric measuring cups, it is important to shake the dry ingredients loosely into the required cup. Do not tap the cup on the bench, or pack the ingredients into the cup unless otherwise directed. Level top of cup with knife. When using graduated metric measuring spoons, level top of spoon with knife. When measuring liquids in the jug, place jug on flat surface, check for accuracy at eye level.

OVEN TEMPERATURES

These oven temperatures are only a guide; we've given you the lower degree of heat. Always check the manufacturer's manual.

	C° (Celsius)	F° (Fahrenheit)	Gas Mark
Very slow	120	250	1
Slow	150	300	2
Moderately slow	160	325	3
Moderate	180 - 190	350 - 375	4
Moderately hot	200 - 210	400 - 425	5
Hot	220 - 230	450 - 475	6
Very hot	240 - 250	500 - 525	7

TWO GREAT OFFERS FROM THE AWW HOME LIBRARY

Here's the perfect way to keep your Home Library books in order, clean and within easy reach. More than a dozen books fit into this smart silver grey vinyl folder. PRICE: Australia $11.95; elsewhere $21.95; prices include postage and handling. To order your holder, see the details below.

All recipes in the AWW Home Library are created using Australia's unique system of metric cups and spoons. While it is relatively easy for overseas readers to make any minor conversions required, it is easier still to own this durable set of Australian cups and spoons (photographed). PRICE : Australia: $5.95; New Zealand: $A8.00; elsewhere: $A9.95; prices include postage & handling.
This offer is available in all countries.

TO ORDER YOUR METRIC MEASURING SET OR BOOK HOLDER:

PHONE: Have your credit card details ready. Sydney: (02) 9260 0035; **elsewhere in Australia:** 1800 252 515 (free call, Mon-Fri, 8.30am-5.30pm) or FAX your order to (02) 9267 4363 or MAIL your order by photocopying or cutting out and completing the coupon below.

PAYMENT: **Australian residents:** We accept the credit cards listed, money orders and cheques. **Overseas residents:** We accept the credit cards listed, drafts in $A drawn on an Australian bank, also English, New Zealand and U.S. cheques in the currency of the country of issue.
Credit card charges are at the exchange rate current at the time of payment.

Please photocopy and complete coupon and fax or send to:
AWW Home Library Reader Offer, ACP Direct, PO Box 7036, Sydney 1028.

❑ Metric Measuring Set   ❑ Holder
Please indicate number(s) required.

Mr/Mrs/Ms _____

Address_____

_____

Postcode _____ Country_____

Ph: *Bus. Hours:*(   )_____

I enclose my cheque/money order for $ _____ payable to ACP Direct
OR: please charge my:
❑ Bankcard ❑ Visa ❑ MasterCard ❑ Diners Club ❑ Amex

| | | | | | | | | | | | | | | | | | | |

Exp. Date _____ / _____

Cardholder's signature _____
(Please allow up to 30 days for delivery within Australia.
Allow up to 6 weeks for overseas deliveries.)
Both offers expire 30/6/98.   HLALL97